This

D1621975

donated by
Harry Zimbler
PSU, MFA '83

LOVE'S FIRE

LOVE'S FIRE

SEVEN NEW PLAYS INSPIRED BY SEVEN SHAKESPEAREAN SONNETS

ORIGINAL WORKS BY

ERIC BOGOSIAN

WILLIAM FINN

JOHN GUARE

TONY KUSHNER

MARSHA NORMAN

NTOZAKE SHANGE

WENDY WASSERSTEIN

INTRODUCTION BY MARK LAMOS

QUILL
WILLIAM MORROW
NEW YORK

ISBN 0-688-16172-3

Printed in the United States of America

BOOK DESIGN BY JO ANNE METSCH
www.williammorrow.com

Love's Fire is dedicated to the memory
of John Houseman, and to the artists and benefactors
who have made his vision of
The Acting Company a reality.

The seven plays in this book were originally commissioned by The Acting Company, a national repertory theater, and produced in association with The Guthrie Theater and the Barbican Centre. *Love's Fire* premiered at The Guthrie Theater Lab in Minneapolis, Minnesota, on January 7, 1998.

Producing Director	Margot Harley
Director	Mark Lamos
Set Designer	Michael Yeargan
Costume Designer	Candice Donnelly
Lighting Designer	Robert Wierzel
Sound Designer	John Gromada
Dramaturge	Anne Cattaneo

INTRODUCTION
by Mark Lamos

We would like to believe that our age is wholly new and that its acts and artifacts are unprecedented; but in fact the old is invariably incorporated into the present. The future is composed by the past, which is both "insidious and reassuring," as one critic once said.

Shakespeare's sonnets are artifacts of the Renaissance, a time when Europe looked both forward and back: forward to the unknowable future, back to the Greeks and the Romans. Whether a Shakespearean sonnet is the product of an imagination or the classically organized detritus of autobiographical events, these particular literary artifacts still throb with anger, remonstrance, lust, forgiveness, and instruction in a way that keeps them evergreen.

An obsession with the autobiographical possibilities of the sonnets, such as conjecture about Shakespeare's involvement with and infatuation for an unidentified man and a "dark lady," can limit their power for a modern reader; appreciation of their variegated texture and multi-meanings can be diminished to hypothetical gossip. Whatever the pain that might have inspired or caused the sonnets, this sequence of 154 poems, rigidly calculated, formally phrased, and surging with violent emotional life continues to define love and emotional trauma with immediacy and ambiguity.

They weren't meant to be read aloud. You can tell that when you compare them to Shakespeare's dramatic sonnets—the meeting of Romeo and Juliet, for instance, or the introductions delivered by the Chorus in *Henry V*—which are intended to prepare an audience for what is about to unfold. Rather, I think of Shakespeare's sonnet sequence as having been designed to be read quietly, by candle light or natural daylight—especially if they were delivered to a chosen recipient. That proved but one of the challenges of *Love's Fire:* incorporating these sonnets spoken by the actors into seven plays whose language is startlingly contemporary.

Sonnet scholar Helen Vendler writes in her scrutiny of the sonnets, "I assume that the features of these poems are designed to cooperate with, reinforce, meaningfully contradict, and play with one another." Similarly, these one-act plays make contact sport with the themes expressed in the Petrarchan sonnet form as rethought by Shakespeare. Vendler assumes "that a poem is not an essay, and that its paraphrasable propositional content is merely the jumping-off place for its real work." Well, consider these seven short plays some of the "real work" of Shakespeare's sonnets.

The one-acts interact with the past and the present. Some of the writers are more literal than others. Dramaturge Anne Cattaneo, who first suggested that The Acting Company's planned commission focus on the sonnets as the inspiration for an evening in the theater, selected the sonnets she thought most compatible with the individual styles of the playwrights; she gave each person the same deadline; no playwright knew what the others were doing. Eric Bogosian's "Bitter Sauce" was the first to arrive, and a complete surprise. After Eric and I met over breakfast in TriBeCa, I had expected a play about the erotic change that comes from studying Shakespeare. Though it took me awhile to come to grips with it, once read aloud, the play clearly succeeded as a hilarious comedy. Marsha Norman's "140" came next, laser-sharp and dark. I remember reading it standing up, unable to sit down and relax, as its pages curled sinuously from my fax machine. Bill Finn definitively howled through his song "Painting You" at least eleven times in the bowels of Lincoln Center. Ntozake Shange's dance poem, "Hydraulics Phat Like Mean," also slithered through my fax machine in Hartford; I found it incomprehensible at first, then realized I had only its first and last pages, and still it began to make complete sense to me only during dress rehearsals in Minneapolis when I saw it interplay with Dyane Harvey's sensuous choreography, a jazz score by the great Chico Freeman, the sexy costumes of Candice Donnelly, John Gromada's in-depth sound design, and finally, the video monitors.

Tony Kushner, who responds to deadlines in a Perils of Pauline sort of way, called from a plane somewhere over my head, on his way between speaking engagements. He was halfway through the process of creation, he said, and he was full of his usual doubts—it was different from anything he'd ever written, he couldn't imagine when he'd finish it, could I substitute another writer and let's call it a day? But then "Terminating . . ." arrived, just past deadline, and when we read it with the actors, it was a completely modern version of Shakespeare's amalgamation of love and need and torment.

Wendy Wasserstein spoke to the actors we had chosen before she began writing. She'd had an idea for a play for some time, she said, and she felt the adaptation of her assigned sonnet might provide a jumping-off spot for a play about the insular world of American movers and shakers, people who are interested only in each other, not in the world at large.

"The General of Hot Desire," John Guare's work, based on the last two sonnets of Shakespeare's sequence, was developed with the company through a number of drafts, each read aloud and partially improvised by John as he worked with us. Composer Adam Guettel was brought into the project, since John was hoping for something operatic in scope. Being a part of its creation was an exhilarating experience, and some of that buoyancy has found its way into the production.

I didn't determine the playing order until we were rehearsing for our first preview at the Guthrie Lab in Minneapolis. "Bitter Sauce" seemed the correct opener right from the start because of its accessibility and comic energy, which I felt would bring the audience, particularly its younger members, right into the production. "The General of Hot Desire," because it was the one play that featured the entire Acting Company ensemble and was about the act of creation, seemed appropriate for the finale. Each play's production had a different gestation period, and each of the playwrights dropped in on rehearsals to approve our approach to interpreting the widely differing tonalities of each work.

The actors were inspiring every inch of the way, and I, accustomed to shaping the long arcs of classic plays by Shakespeare, Ibsen, Shaw, and Molière, delighted in these pungent bytes of theater. Each from a different pen, they "meaningfully contradict" each other and provide a whole new insight into the everlasting power of these amazing sonnets, more than four hundred years old.

Contents

Bitter Sauce

 ERIC BOGOSIAN

INSPIRED BY SHAKESPEARE'S SONNET 118

CHARACTERS

A couch in the midst of the small living room of a small apartment. On the couch sits RENGIN, a beautiful young woman, in a white wedding gown. She is drinking from a pint flask of bourbon. The phone rings. She doesn't bother with it. Instead, she rises unsteadily and checks herself out in a mirror.

A voice can be heard on the message machine.

HERMAN *(voice):* Rengin, it's me. Are you there? Please pick up if you are. Rengin? I'm sorry. Whatever I did. I'm such an ass. Please pick up. Please? OK. I'm coming home. I'm actually downstairs. If you are there, don't be surprised when you see me. Maybe you're in the bathroom. Then I understand why you're not picking up.

RENGIN has walked over to the answering machine and is watching it record the message.

RENGIN: Herman, you don't get it. You never got it.

She goes back to the mirror.

RENGIN: What is this I am wearing? A white dress. Meaning what? Virginity? That the male proboscis has not slid through my vaginal lips? What bullshit! *(drinks)* What the fuck am I here? A human sacrifice? I am a womb being readied for impalement and fertilization. Yech!!!

She touches the bodice, feels it, as she drinks.

RENGIN: But I can't take it off. I'm drunk as shit and I can't take it off. He's got to see me like this. We should go out together like this. Maybe someplace that has a mosh pit. I should mosh in my wedding dress and then find some bikers and have three guys screw me at the same time. And make Herman watch. Prepare him . . .

She drinks and wails.

RENGIN: FUCKING "A," MAN, HOW THE FUCK DID THIS *HAPPEN*?

HERMAN enters.

HERMAN: Rengin, what's wrong? Why didn't you answer the phone?

RENGIN: I'm getting shit-faced.

HERMAN: Why, honey? *(guesses)* You don't like your wedding gown.

RENGIN: No, I don't like my wedding gown. Hey, I have an idea. You wear the wedding gown and I'll wear the tux. And then when we go on our honeymoon I'll fuck you. How about that?

HERMAN: I think you're drunk.

RENGIN: No shit, Sherlock.

HERMAN: Why don't we go to bed? Tomorrow's a new day. C'mon.

RENGIN takes a long look at HERMAN.

RENGIN: You want some of this?

HERMAN: No. Thanks.

RENGIN: What do you want?

HERMAN: I just want to be with you, Rengin. To love you and take care of you.

RENGIN: Why?

HERMAN: Because you're you.

RENGIN: Uh-huh.

HERMAN: Are we going to start this now? Again?

RENGIN deflates.

RENGIN: It's not your fault. It's *my* fault. Everything's fucked up and it's my fault. I'm afraid, I'm afraid of you.

HERMAN: Why are you afraid of me?

RENGIN: Because you actually love me. With real love, not pornographic, catch-the-prize love.

HERMAN: And don't you love me?

RENGIN: No. No. You're right. Let's go to bed. I love you too, Herman. I really do. If we both died tonight, like Romeo and Juliet, that wouldn't be so bad, would it?

HERMAN: It would be great.

RENGIN: I really fucked up this time.

HERMAN: Hey, we all have our faults. I'm no saint.

RENGIN: You're not? I thought you were.

HERMAN: *(small smile)* Why don't you take the wedding gown off so it isn't all wrinkled tomorrow? They cost a lot to dry clean. And then you tell me what's bothering you.

HERMAN unzips the back.

RENGIN: Yeah . . . I do love you, you know. Whatever happens.

RENGIN starts to walk off. Then stops, hands HERMAN the bottle.

RENGIN: Here.

She kisses him. Then she walks off into another room, removing her dress.

RENGIN *(offstage)*: *(frustrated)* AARRRGGGGHHHHH!!!!!

HERMAN is left holding the bottle. He smells it, puts it away somewhere. He checks his watch. He sits in a chair and takes his shoes off.

RENGIN reenters, slipping on a bathrobe.

RENGIN: Herman, sit down over here on the couch for a sec. I have to tell you something.

HERMAN: Yeah? What?

RENGIN: *(looks around)* Where'd the bottle go?

HERMAN: I put it away.

RENGIN: OK. OK. *(sorting her thoughts)* Listen, Herman. You're a nice guy.

HERMAN: Oh no.

RENGIN: What?

HERMAN: You're gonna start this, "You're a nice guy—I'm a shit," routine again. Tell me how you're no good for me.

RENGIN: No, no, listen. Well, I am no good for you . . . uh you know how sometimes something bad will happen and you figure, why worry about it, it'll probably go away? . . . shit . . . I *SUCK*!!!!

HERMAN: Listen, Rengin, I love you. As they say, "Warts and all."

RENGIN: What warts?

HERMAN: You don't have any warts, I'm just saying.

RENGIN: No, wait, wait. I know I have warts. I've got warts that are the size of mountains. I just wish you had some, because I gotta tell you this.

HERMAN: OK, what?

RENGIN: Remember when we first started going out?

HERMAN: Oh yeah.

RENGIN: And that first two weeks we were floating on air? We talked every night on the phone. You took me to Bouley. You slipped a five to the maitre d'? I'd never been with a guy cool enough to do that.

HERMAN: I read about it in a book.

RENGIN: And we had that amazing boat ride on the ferry? And we got drunk and then we came home and you were so amazing. You just didn't seem like an all-night guy to me.

HERMAN: I couldn't get enough of you.

RENGIN: That's for sure. I couldn't walk for two days.

HERMAN: And I thought, "What is she doing with a nothing like me?"

RENGIN: OK, right, I thought the same thing. He's so smart

and so sweet and handsome. And a surprisingly great lay. And has a job and everything.

HERMAN: And six months later we're getting married. If you want to wait, to be really sure, it's OK with me. Whatever you want.

RENGIN: No, wait, wait, *wait*. This is kind of bigger than that.

HERMAN: Bigger than our wedding?

RENGIN: *(She melts a bit.)* Oh . . . Wait so, but when we first started going out, it was like *too* good. I kept thinking "Where's the catch?" And I thought, "I'm falling too fast for this guy. I'm going to hit the ground and I'm going to break every bone in my body." You know what I'm saying?

HERMAN: Well, I didn't see it in such a dramatic way, but yes, I felt the same thing. It was intense. It still is.

RENGIN: Yeah. Yeah, it *is*. That's the weird part. It's getting more intense all the time. I mean, if I ever thought you would leave me . . .

HERMAN: Never . . .

RENGIN: Or if anything ever happened to you . . .

HERMAN: Come on . . .

RENGIN: I think I would flip out. And I've never felt that way about a guy, a man, before. Never. You're like too good to be true.

HERMAN: Can I just say something here? I feel exactly the same way about you. It's love, right? Real love. I think most people have fake love. But we're lucky. We have the real thing.

RENGIN: Yeah, that's the problem.

HERMAN: Why, because fear is part of it? That's life, kid. To have something wonderful means you might lose it.

RENGIN: Yeah, but Herman . . .

HERMAN: What?

RENGIN: There were other guys.

HERMAN: This is news?

RENGIN: No, I mean . . . see . . . since I thought I was going to get crushed by you, I mean, I had no idea what was going on. Since I was sure that it was too good, too intense, I needed something to ground me.

HERMAN: You were seeing another guy while we were going out?

RENGIN: Sort of. I mean, my heart was not into it in any way whatsoever. It was just an insurance policy . . .

HERMAN gets up, finds the bottle of bourbon and takes a slug.

RENGIN: I don't really have to tell you this.

HERMAN: I'm a nice guy, Rengin, but I'm not a wimp. Tell me.

RENGIN: I don't *want* to tell you this.

HERMAN: Rengin, you've got me all interested now.

RENGIN: I was in this bar one night, getting shit-faced because I was so in love with you and it felt so weird and I, well, I figured the best antidote to how intense our love was, was something just as intense, but in the other direction.

HERMAN: "Other direction."

RENGIN: Let me finish. So I'm sitting there, thinking this, and this biker guy, "Red," sits down next to me. I figure it was fate. So I hung out with him for a while.

HERMAN: "A while."

RENGIN: See, I don't love him. But uh, he loves me. In his own way. He's like your opposite. He throws me around. He's into rough sex.

HERMAN: "Rough sex."

RENGIN: It's just sex, Herman. . . . And that's pretty much the whole story.

HERMAN: "Pretty much"?

RENGIN: Well, we shot dope together a couple of times. Smoked some crack. And oh yeah, he never listens to me.

HERMAN: Wow. This *is* news. How long did this go on?

RENGIN: Well, I haven't seen him for . . . about three days.

HERMAN: WHAT??????

RENGIN: Because I love *you*. See? I love you so much that I needed this monster in my life, just in case . . .

HERMAN: You need him because he *hurts* you?

RENGIN: No, it's not like that old cliché. I only love you.

HERMAN: But you've been seeing him, too?

RENGIN: No, listen. I *don't* see him. He sees *me*. Once you and I were really happening, I told Red I couldn't see him anymore. That was like four months ago. But, uh, he's hard to convince.

HERMAN: So he forces himself on you?

RENGIN: Well, that was kind of the deal in the first place. He's an animal, Herman. He's the kind of guy who starts fights and hopes that the cops show up so he can fight them, too.

HERMAN: So what happens now?

RENGIN: Well, I told him I was getting married.

HERMAN: And?

RENGIN: He thought that was great. Said he'd come by the night before and give me a good-bye fuck. And then he plans to stop by once a week to get his pipes cleaned.

HERMAN: This is criminal.

RENGIN: Yeah, but *I* started it. I needed like an antidote. . . .

HERMAN takes another drink.

HERMAN: So just tell him you won't see him anymore.

RENGIN: Honey, you want to be married to a woman with all her teeth?

HERMAN: You said, "the night before." That's tonight.

RENGIN: Uh-huh.

HERMAN: Tonight. Like now.

RENGIN: Uh-huh.

HERMAN: That's why you're getting drunk.

RENGIN: Uh-huh.

HERMAN: I will tell him that it's over between you and him.

RENGIN throws herself on HERMAN.

RENGIN: No!!! You can't.

HERMAN: Why, do you still love him?

RENGIN: I *never* loved him, you idiot. I love you. That's why I don't want to see you mashed into Herman-burger.

There's a knock at the front door.

RENGIN: Oh shit.

HERMAN: I will tell him.

RENGIN: No, baby, he'll peel your skin off. He'll make a saddlebag out of you and hang you off the side of his Harley.

HERMAN: He has a Harley?

RENGIN: Of course, he's a *biker*.

HERMAN: Go in the bedroom.

RENGIN: No . . . please.

HERMAN: Go in the bedroom or I'm calling the wedding off. And I don't care what my mother says.

RENGIN reluctantly goes to the bedroom. Hesitates.

RENGIN: Promise me that if he starts to kill you you'll jump out the window or something.

HERMAN: Go.

RENGIN goes into the bedroom and closes the door. HERMAN opens the front door to find RED, a meaty, furry guy standing there.

RED: The fuck?

HERMAN: Yes?

RED: *(striding into the room)* Where's Rengin?

HERMAN: She's not here.

RED: Who are you?

HERMAN: I'm her fiancé. Herman.

RED: Yeah?

HERMAN: Yes.

RED: Fuck.

HERMAN: Who are you?

RED: Red. Motor Captain. North Reading Chapter, Hell's Angels. So where is she?

HERMAN: She's dead.

RED: Say what?

HERMAN: She died. Three days ago.

RED: I just saw her three days ago.

HERMAN: Something happened to her. The police aren't sure. She died . . . from contusions. They're looking for a biker.

RED: *(suspicious)* Contusions?

HERMAN: Yes. Very bad. The police said she had had "rough sex."

RED: Wow. She's dead.

HERMAN: Yes.

RED: You're her boyfriend, right?

HERMAN: Yes.

RED: So why aren't you sad?

HERMAN: I am sad.

After a pause, RED gets into it.

RED: Me, too. I'm sad, too.

HERMAN: Well, so . . . I'm sorry but I have to go meet my mother . . . so . . .

RED spies the whiskey bottle. Grabs it.

RED: A toast to Rengin!

HERMAN doesn't have much choice.

HERMAN: A toast.

RED: A great piece of ass.

RED drinks and passes it to Herman.

HERMAN: A great piece of ass.

HERMAN takes a hit.

RED: She told me about you.

HERMAN: Really?

RED: Yeah. She said you were a "stabilizing influence." Whatever the fuck that means.

HERMAN: That's nice of her to say that.

RED: She said things with me were so intense, she needed someone to bring her back to earth. Like you were an "antidote" or something.

HERMAN: She said that?

RED: What?

HERMAN: That I was an antidote?

RED: Something like that.

HERMAN is now truly sorrowful.

HERMAN: She told me she loved me.

HERMAN sits.

RED consoles Herman.

RED: She did. She did. But bitches are bitches. You know what I'm saying?

HERMAN: I don't know about bitches. I thought I knew about Rengin.

RED: Well she's gone and we'll miss her. What else can you say?

The gears are turning in HERMAN's fevered brow.

HERMAN: You killed her.

RED: Me?

HERMAN: You beat her up and you killed her.

RED: You're dreaming, pal.

HERMAN: She was a wonderful girl and you defiled her. And you killed her. And now I don't have her anymore.

RED: So?

HERMAN gets a wild look in his eyes.

HERMAN: So now I'm gonna kill you. Maybe not right now. But I will track you down and make you pay.

RED: *(smiles)* How you plan to do that?

HERMAN: I'll think of something.

RED is a little wary of HERMAN. Something about him is spooky.

RED: *(weaker smile)* You have to find me.

HERMAN: How hard can that be?

RED: Good luck, pal. Good fucking luck.

HERMAN: That's it?

RED: What?

HERMAN: You come into my life and ruin it and leave and it's "Good luck, pal"?

RED: You're better off this way. I did you a favor, pal. You got your head up your ass. When you get around to pulling it out, you'll realize that there ain't no such thing as love, not with Rengin, not with anybody. There's only the battle. And in every battle, only one person wins.

HERMAN: Well, I'm gonna win. I'm going to stalk you for the rest of your days.

RED: No you're not. Cause I'm out of here. Nice knowing you.

HERMAN: I'll find you. The cops will find you. *"Contusions."*

RED: Listen, big guy, I'm walking out this door. If you even try to get near me, anywhere, anyplace, I will carve you so many new assholes you . . . you . . . *(Red can't think of a punchline.)*

HERMAN: *(emboldened with madness)* What? What, "BIG GUY"?

RED: *(moving to the door)* Just . . . just . . . stay away from me.

HERMAN: You're dead.

RED scoots out the door. RENGIN emerges from the bedroom.

RENGIN: That was amazing.

HERMAN: *(cool)* Yeah?

RENGIN: You made him go away. *Permanently.* You tricked him. You're a genius! Oh, Herman, I love you!

RENGIN tries to embrace HERMAN, but he backs off, still full of energy.

HERMAN: But those things he said.

RENGIN: It's all bullshit.

HERMAN: Is it?

RENGIN: Hey. It's *me*, remember?

HERMAN: You?

RENGIN: The woman you love.

HERMAN: But, Rengin . . .

RENGIN: I made a mistake. I'm human.

HERMAN: There are mistakes and there are mistakes.

RENGIN: Look, Herman, this is a dead end. If you like getting your back scratched, you're gonna get bitten now and then.

HERMAN: *(suddenly meek)* I like both those things.

RENGIN: I know you do.

She strokes his hair.

HERMAN: *(pouting)* But you were bad. You cuckolded me. We could have been killed.

RENGIN: That was then, this is now. OK?

HERMAN: (pause) OK.

RENGIN: C'mon . . .

BLACKOUT

Like as, to make our appetites more keen,
With eager compounds we our palate urge;
As, to prevent our maladies unseen,
We sicken to shun sickness when we purge:
Even so, being full of your ne'er-cloying sweetness,
To bitter sauces did I frame my feeding;
And, sick of welfare, found a kind of meetness
To be diseas'd ere that there was true needing.
Thus policy in love, t'anticipate
The ills that were not, grew to faults assured,
And brought to medicine a healthful state,
Which, rank of goodness, would by ill be cured.
    But thence I learn, and find the lesson true,
    Drugs poison him that so fell sick of you.

HYDRAULICS PHAT
LIKE MEAN

NTOZAKE SHANGE

INSPIRED BY SHAKESPEARE'S SONNET 128

ORIGINAL MUSIC BY CHICO FREEMAN

CHOREOGRAPHY BY DYANE HARVEY

CHARACTERS

FEMALE PLAYER .... *Lisa Tharps*

MALE PLAYER .... *Jason Alan Carvell*

SONNET 128 .... *Jason Alan Carvell*

We hear music which varies in texture from hip-hop to traditional rhythms in which melody already exits.

FEMALE PLAYER enters dancing in a manner that will set her up to fall into playing the instrument of choice. She is involved in the seduction of the audience as the music we hear seduces her. MALE PLAYER responds with his body, so that the language is virtually forced from him by the power of the woman and the music combined.

MALE PLAYER: Couldn't you bring yourself to make me sound like that? To let me feel the magic of whatever you do . . . *(FEMALE PLAYER intensifies playing of instrument suggesting Cecil Taylor. The male responds physically, incontrovertibly possessed. He calms as the music calms and the female is obviously satisfied with her powers.)* Yes. Yes, something like that. Isn't there a sacred word you whisper, some phrase, or chant you use to . . . make noise into what is more lovely than Hale-Bopp? *(She retorts in staccato. He is beaten down again.)* No. No. Silence is not an appropriate example, but the lights your body dazzles with, the fireworks you, who can only be music, at least to me, my song . . . *(She becomes agitated again. His body is thrown to the floor and around until she has worked through her displeasure.)*

MALE PLAYER: *(sings)* "Mil razones para amarte / y tu eres la primera / mil poemas en la calle / yo rondo donde quieras."

They dance together. Paso Doble. Or simply mirror-movement suggesting an emotional cohesion that could be love. She stops suddenly and goes back to playing the instrument. He is spent, listless.

FEMALE PLAYER: *(slowing, finding some blues standard)* All you got to do is, say, give me an "A," Daddy. *(She continues to play.)*

MALE PLAYER: I could do that for you. *(indicating becoming "the music")*

Female coyly ignores him. In true chivalric fashion of the streets, say, late fifties or the present manner of R. Kelly or "Babyface," MALE PLAYER approaches her.

FEMALE PLAYER: You think so?

MALE PLAYER: Oh yes, baby. Querida. Mi jeba. *(carried away with anticipation of pleasures)* You could stop all that/let my fingers sail your inlets and bays. *(FEMALE PLAYER plays instrument a bit out of control in response to these love entreaties.)* Have you ever felt yourself to be high tide? Can you hear the thrashing, the ebb . . . ? See where our toes dig deep in wet sands, only disappearing if we move.

FEMALE PLAYER: *(An arpeggio that slows to minimal sounds, very soft. She is touched. She is moved. Her body takes on the rhythm of the sea. The MALE PLAYER takes pleasure in this, but in this, minds not to get too close, lest she drift away from him.)* Motion is inevitable.

MALE PLAYER: You are definitely correct. No doubt about it. Why I sometimes must keep my very self from jumping out all over the place. *(Obviously he tries to mask his erection or the thought of it coming unexpectedly.)*

FEMALE PLAYER: So I see.

MALE PLAYER: You do? Oh, mi cielo, my darlin' darlin' baby, if only I could find your 6/8 or 3/4, the flow of you in my arms, do you know what I mean? I want, no, I need to blend with your meters. Is that the right term, meter?

FEMALE PLAYER: Aren't you aiming a bit low? You have to know what key I sing in before any of that. No, it is not meter. Meters indicate distance and I am virtually on top of you.

MALE PLAYER: Would that you were?

FEMALE PLAYER: I'm sorry. I didn't catch that last. . . . Could you repeat that?

MALE PLAYER: Oh, if only you'd let me.

FEMALE PLAYER: What?

MALE PLAYER: Repeat . . . that.

FEMALE PLAYER: Then go ahead. What's stopping you?

MALE PLAYER: Well *(indicating the instrument)*, you seem otherwise engaged. I mean to say, how can I possibly intrigue you as much as that thing? *(disdainfully)*

FEMALE PLAYER: *(a little confused and hurt)* All that is here is me. *(She plays something beautiful and light.)*

MALE PLAYER: What if I were to lie before you, totally open to your touch, your fingers a fantastical breeze upon my back letting the willow sigh by the brook, the basketball rhumba, the slide of skateboards careen by my cheek, what if your fingers found music, here, in me.

FEMALE PLAYER: That ain't no thing my "C. C. Rider," mi vida, sugar pie honey bunch. But, it's not the secret. *(sweetly)*

MALE PLAYER: No?

FEMALE PLAYER: No. *(playing her instrument with concentration)*

MALE PLAYER: What am I missin'?

FEMALE PLAYER: Listen.

MALE PLAYER: What'd you mean "listen"? That's all I can do is listen to you. Hear you cruising my limbs like a canary low-rider by San Pedro, so wild at the stoplight bouncing to the beat, up and down 'n' all around. Can't you just see yourself, top down, hydraulics phat like mean, dancing to the song of yourself, you woman, can you hear me? Do you understand what I'm saying to you?

FEMALE PLAYER: Yeah, you want me to let you ride in my car that I worked so hard on, let vatos laugh at me till I learned the mystery of my own mechanical systems. Complex, my brother-man. Takes a learned touch. Haven't you seen them ads on the television? "Don't pick up strangers . . . less you know them."

MALE PLAYER: Why do you taunt me so? You tryin' to make me feel less than a man? I gotta learned touch. Shit. I got the fingers of Hilton Ruiz, Jimi Hendrix, and Olatunji. What you got to say to that?

FEMALE PLAYER: *(Does not respond. Goes back to playing her instrument. The saxophone or solo instrument that preceded their entrance comes up on her last lines.)* I'm waitin' for you.

MALE PLAYER: Waitin' for me?

FEMALE PLAYER: UM-humm.

MALE PLAYER: Waitin'. (*Looks around himself, exasperated.*)
Waitin' for what? What more do you want from me?

FEMALE PLAYER: I want to hear you.

MALE PLAYER: I've been pourin' my heart out to you, girl.
I never talk to nobody like I been talkin' to you.

FEMALE PLAYER: Humm.

MALE PLAYER: Whatchu talkin' 'bout "hum"?

FEMALE PLAYER: For you to be.

MALE PLAYER: Como yo no estoy aquí. Like I'm not here
in front of you?

FEMALE PLAYER: Beside me.

MALE PLAYER: You are startin' to get to me, now. (*agitated*)

FEMALE PLAYER: Good. Let go.

MALE PLAYER: Let go? Let go of what?

FEMALE PLAYER: Let go of some of my music you took
from me?

MALE PLAYER: I ain't got your music, woman.

FEMALE PLAYER: I know. (*She plays furiously.*)

MALE PLAYER: Then, what do you want?

FEMALE PLAYER: Some of yours. (*Smiles. Stops playing. His
saxophone solo comes up. He moves toward her. She plays with
the saxophone. Their bodies become entangled in the playing of
the music. The lights fade as they move to kiss, but go to black
before the kiss is actually executed.*)

THE END

How oft, when thou, my music, music play'st
Upon that blessed wood whose motion sounds
With thy sweet fingers when thou gently sway'st
The wiry concord that mine ear confounds,
Do I envy those jacks that nimble leap
To kiss the tender inward of thy hand,
Whilst my poor lips, which should that harvest reap,
At the wood's boldness by thee blushing stand!
To be so tickled, they would change their state
And situation with those dancing chips,
O'er whom thy fingers walk with gentle gait,
Making dead wood more blest than living lips.
   Since saucy jacks so happy are in this,
   Give them thy fingers, me, thy lips, to kiss.

140

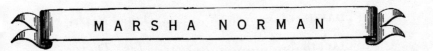

MARSHA NORMAN

INSPIRED BY SHAKESPEARE'S SONNET 140

CHARACTERS

WIFE.................................. *Jennifer Rohn*

DAVID................................. *Daniel Pearce*

JACKIE .... *Lisa Tharps*

ROLAND .... *Hamish Linklater*

ROLAND'S NEW LOVER......... *James Farmer*

ROLAND'S LOVER'S NEW LOVER..... *Heather Robison*

ROLAND'S NEW LOVER'S LOVER......... *Jason Alan Carvell*

LOVER.............................. *Stephen DeRosa*

LOVER.............................. *Erika Rolfsrud*

SONNET 140 .... *Stephen DeRosa and Heather Robison*

People stand quietly against the upstage wall. In something of a line.

Center stage, DAVID sits in a chair, his jacket half off, as though undressing, but not.

His WIFE circles him as she talks. When he can manage it, he casts a longing glance at his young lover, who stands just to the side, listening but not present.

After a moment, she begins.

WIFE: This wasn't smart. Why weren't you smart about this.

He starts to speak.

WIFE: No, no. I don't need you to say anything.

He starts to get up.

WIFE: Just sit there.

He sits.

WIFE: I know about . . . about you and . . .

She nods in the direction of the lover.

WIFE: Jackie. I know where you go, and how long you stay there. I practically know what you do to each other. I know everything.

She takes a moment. Then casually —

WIFE: Except how it feels, of course.

He begins to speak. She stops him.

WIFE: No, no. We'll assume it feels good. We'll just presume you get so-o-o lost, you forget where you are, *who* you are—who *cares* who you are. You think you're going to die. You *wish* you would, too, don't you, because it's all really going to be downhill after this, isn't it. Man alive.

He looks away. She changes direction.

WIFE: You didn't know you still had it in you.

A moment.

WIFE: But you do.

A moment.

WIFE: I could've told you that. If—

He begins to lean toward JACKIE. His WIFE fights her despair.

WIFE: If you had any . . . if you knew how these things were done . . . you would just walk right in the door right now and—

She begins to lose it.

WIFE: Tell me you love me. *(to herself)* Stupid. I know it's stupid. *(to him)* I'm serious. You should walk right in the door and convince me you love me.

DAVID can't believe what he has heard.

WIFE: Like a doctor would if I were dying. If I'm dying . . . when I'm dying? Tell the doctor to tell me how great I look, OK? I don't want to be told I'm *dying.* I know I'm dying. I'm the one doing the dying. The first day I knew you, I knew you would betray me. *(pause)* Water under the bridge. OK.

He looks away.

WIFE: Tell me that you love me and we'll start there.

He starts to speak, but his attention is drawn to JACKIE, who has turned to look at him.

WIFE: David. Just tell me you love me and we'll start over.

JACKIE comes toward him, beginning to undress slightly, unbuttoning something, or stepping out of her skirt.

WIFE: Otherwise . . .

DAVID extends his hand to JACKIE.

WIFE: Otherwise I will go mad.

He pulls JACKIE down into a kiss. We realize DAVID is not in the room with his WIFE at all. He is with JACKIE.

WIFE: I will go mad.

DAVID strokes JACKIE's face. His WIFE watches, going mad.

WIFE: And when anyone asks, I will tell them where you are, and what you are doing, which won't be far from the truth. Not too far. He is in her bed, in her mouth, in her hair. All day, all night. He comes home and he can't even speak. He comes to me and he doesn't say a thing. And pretty soon, David, they won't even see *you*. They'll see you shaking with the pleasure of her. They will feel her. They will taste her. And they will hate you. *(a moment)* Hate you.

The lover stands.

WIFE: And . . . *(She considers.)* They will abandon you to your pleasure. *(a moment)* And comfort me.

There is a long moment.

WIFE: *(composing herself)* Unless.

JACKIE takes a few steps away. DAVID stands and finally looks at his wife.

WIFE: You could stop staring at her, I suppose, and I could hold my tongue. And—

He straightens his jacket.

WIFE: We could be exactly who we were. *(He looks up.)* You could be tall and proud and handsome and every good thing. *(He smiles, as though being introduced.)* And I could just stand it. Stand here, I mean. I could just stand it.

She looks straight at him. And there is a pause.

But when DAVID doesn't respond, his WIFE walks upstage and goes to the end of the line of people standing along the wall.

There is a sense of time passing, all too quickly.

JACKIE, who has not left the stage, now comes to sit in the chair where DAVID was before. She is still half undressed.

After a moment, ROLAND, her new lover, appears. She looks at him, melting in unsmiling submission.

DAVID sees the whole thing. He is furious.

DAVID: No. Not you talk. Me. You just sit there and shut up.

She starts to say something.

DAVID: But you even think about feeling sorry for me and I'll kill you. No, I'm not kidding. How long has this been going on? Such a fucking fool. How many of us have you had, huh? *(to himself but no less intense)* Stop it. Stop calling her names. *(to her)* I'm sorry. What didn't I do? Not the right thing, obviously, like you had any idea what that was. Was there anything I could've done to please you? I doubt it. Look. I loved you. That was my excuse.

She starts to leave.

DAVID: OK. OK. All I ask . . . all I ask is . . . can we just be smart about this? I mean, we don't have to humiliate each other. Because believe me, if you make me look stupid here, I won't have any choice. I'll say whatever I have to say to come out on top of this thing, and you know where that leaves you, baby.

She looks away.

DAVID: Baby, baby. Don't make me be this way. You love me. I know you love me. Tell me you love me, baby. Tell me you didn't care about this other man. Woman, whoever the hell it was. Tell me it was just that one time. I want something I can believe, OK? That's all I want.

I want to believe we had something. More than the physical thing, I mean. Not that the physical thing wasn't great. It was great. Wasn't it great? You have no right to treat me like this. Not to talk to me like this.

JACKIE extends her hand to ROLAND. He smiles and approaches, loosening his tie or in some other way beginning to undress.

DAVID: OK. Jackie. It's OK. You want to have other people. Have other people. Just have them in some other city, OK?

JACKIE pulls ROLAND down into a kiss. We realize she is not in the room with DAVID at all. She is with ROLAND.

DAVID: You want me to say please. I'll say please. You come home and I'll say please.

JACKIE looks up at him. Bids ROLAND a fond farewell, as though fully expecting to see him later.

DAVID: Or. How about if we don't talk about it at all. OK? I won't say . . . any of this.

JACKIE stands.

DAVID: You'll just agree that whenever we're in the same room with one of your lovers, you won't look at them. That will work, I think. OK. Good.

JACKIE walks up to him, clasps his hand and smiles. Then after a moment, they part.

Then DAVID walks far upstage and takes his place beside his WIFE.

JACKIE expects ROLAND to come to her, but instead, he walks over to sit in the chair. His eyes and heart turning to ice.

ROLAND begins to undress as he stares at his new lover who has moved from the front of the upstage line to stage left.

JACKIE: What are you doing? What are you doing?

ROLAND: I'm tired. I'm going to bed.

JACKIE: Tired of what.

ROLAND: Don't do this.

JACKIE: Tired from what, is more like it. Tired from what, Roland.

ROLAND: I think you already know.

JACKIE: Say it.

ROLAND: So you can hate me?

JACKIE: What did I do?

ROLAND: It wasn't you.

JACKIE: I would've done whatever you wanted.

ROLAND: *(carefully)* It wasn't *what* I wanted. It was who. It wasn't what I wanted someone to do. It was who I wanted to do it. To me. With me.

JACKIE: Not me.

ROLAND: No. Not you. I'm sorry.

JACKIE: You couldn't help it.

ROLAND: Maybe I could. I probably could. But I didn't. I didn't help it.

There is silence. ROLAND'S LOVER'S NEW LOVER appears.

JACKIE: You're going to be sorry, Roland.

ROLAND: I'm already sorry. What am I supposed to do.

JACKIE: Undo it. You're supposed to undo it.

ROLAND'S NEW LOVER: *(to ROLAND)* You want me to undo it.

ROLAND: Yes.

ROLAND'S LOVER'S NEW LOVER: *(to ROLAND'S NEW LOVER)* Undo this.

ROLAND'S NEW LOVER: Yes.

ROLAND: *(to JACKIE)* Shall I undo this?

JACKIE: *(to ROLAND)* Yes.

ROLAND: Now?

JACKIE: Now. *(then turning to DAVID)* Undo this.

DAVID: *(to JACKIE)* This? You want me to undo this?

JACKIE: Can you?

DAVID: My pleasure.

JACKIE: Now. Undo it now.

DAVID: And this?

JACKIE: And this.

ROLAND'S NEW LOVER'S LOVER: *(to DAVID'S WIFE)* Yes?

WIFE: Undo this for me, can you?

ROLAND'S NEW LOVER'S LOVER: Undo this for you. And this.

WIFE: And this. Could you . . . undo . . . all this for me.

ROLAND'S NEW LOVER'S LOVER comes to the WIFE and begins unbuttoning her blouse or taking down her hair. The others move far upstage. Lights dim.

THE END

Be wise as thou art cruel: do not press
My tongue-tied patience with too much disdain;
Lest sorrow lend me words, and words express
The manner of my pity-wanting pain.
If I might teach thee wit, better it were,
Though not to love, yet, love, to tell me so;
As testy sick men, when their deaths be near,
No news but health from their physicians know.
For if I should despair, I should grow mad,
And in my madness might speak ill of thee.
Now this ill-wresting world is grown so bad,
Mad slanderers by mad ears believed be.
    That I may not be so, nor thou belied,
    Bear thine eyes straight, though thy proud heart go
        wide.

Terminating, or Lass Meine Schmerzen Nicht Verloren Sein, or Ambivalence

 TONY KUSHNER

INSPIRED BY SHAKESPEARE'S SONNET 75

CHARACTERS

HENDRYK .... *Stephen DeRosa*

ESTHER .... *Erika Rolfsrud*

DYMPHNA .... *Lisa Tharps*

BILLYGOAT .... *Hamish Linklater*

SONNET 75 .... *Daniel Pearce, Lisa Tharps,
and Hamish Linklater*

ESTHER is an analyst, and this is her office, a chair and a couch. HENDRYK sits on the couch, he does not lie on the couch. ESTHER and HENDRYK are roughly the same age. ESTHER is nicely turned out, HENDRYK is a godforsaken mess. DYMPHNA, ESTHER's younger domestic partner, sits in a chair near ESTHER. BILLYGOAT, HENDRYK's erstwhile much-more-attractive lover, sits near the couch.

HENDRYK: I've gained twenty-four pounds.

ESTHER: Hendryk.

HENDRYK: Last night on the subway I urinated.

ESTHER: Hendryk.

HENDRYK: In my pants.

ESTHER: Hendryk.

HENDRYK: Bladder, um, bladder control, loss of, sudden loss of . . . Waters breaking, whoosh! Drenched!

ESTHER: Hendryk.

HENDRYK: I'm broke.

ESTHER: Hendryk.

HENDRYK: I spent all my money on these . . . these . . . these . . .

ESTHER: Hendryk.

HENDRYK: I . . . *(He waits for the "Hendryk." It doesn't come.)* I, I didn't *need* them, it was just, they're . . . Drapes. It was an idea I had, to, to sew real, uh real, uh *actual* chicken feathers . . .

ESTHER: Hendryk.

HENDRYK: . . . Quilted, sort of, big squares between sheets of sheer, um, *raw* . . . silk. *(He waits for the "Hendryk." It doesn't come so he says:)*

Hendryk.

I find I'm saying *raw* a lot these days, raw silk, raw . . . um, burlap steak wound meat eat me raw the, the raw truth. Raw and, um, *rank*. Rank . . . *betrayal*.

ESTHER: Hen . . .

HENDRYK: All this coil is long of you. Mistress. As they say. *RAW*. Not like I'm not perfectly contented to be free of this room and the constraints of your ultimate indifference to the, uh, the uhhhhh, the.

Pause

ESTHER: Hendryk.

HENDRYK: I want to come back.

ESTHER: No.

HENDRYK: Why not?

ESTHER: I . . .

HENDRYK: Why?

ESTHER: We terminated.

HENDRYK: So?

ESTHER: You . . .

Because.

HENDRYK: What?

ESTHER: You frighten me.

HENDRYK: You're not supposed to say things like that. You're not supposed to say anything, really.

ESTHER: I can say anything I want, Hendryk, you're not my patient anymore.

HENDRYK: But still.

ESTHER: Well you do frighten me.

HENDRYK: I am in love with you.

ESTHER: Transference.

HENDRYK: I don't believe in transference.

ESTHER: Uh huh.

HENDRYK: *All* love is transference. Breast, mom, every fucking other fucking . . .

ESTHER: Hendryk.

HENDRYK: I love you.

ESTHER: Hendryk, you do not, I mean . . .

HENDRYK: I do. It's not . . .

ESTHER: Hendryk, I . . .

HENDRYK: . . . transference.

ESTHER: I HAVE PROBLEMS OF MY OWN, HENDRYK! PROBLEMS! PROBLEMS!

DYMPHNA: I thought you terminated with him. Tell him to leave. Is it bad today?

HENDRYK: This isn't going well and perhaps I should . . .

Pause

ESTHER: I should not have said that you frighten me.

HENDRYK: Countertransference.

ESTHER: Well . . .

HENDRYK: Unanalyzed countertransference.

Pause

HENDRYK: What?

ESTHER: It . . .

HENDRYK: Oh. It's . . . *not* counter . . . So, it's . . . what? *Reality?*

ESTHER: Hendryk.

HENDRYK: I *am*, I mean I actually *am* . . . *frightening?* I mean, *me?*

Pause

HENDRYK: I. Um. The. Um. A-ha. A . . . ha. Wow.

ESTHER: How would it make you feel if I said you were frightening?

HENDRYK: But you did say that.

ESTHER: And how did . . .

HENDRYK: No if.

ESTHER: But how . . .

HENDRYK: No hypothetical.

ESTHER: But.

HENDRYK: You *said* it.

Sleep with me. At least.

ESTHER: *(laughs)* You're gay.

HENDRYK: Oh yeah, well, so what. Gay. What. Is. That. You're a dyke, I'm gay, so . . .

ESTHER: Actually I never said I was a . . .

HENDRYK: Oh come on.

ESTHER: What?

HENDRYK: You wear . . . *Harley Davidson boots* and you have short hair.

ESTHER: Once I wore those boots.

HENDRYK: We saw each other for . . .

ESTHER: You were my patient.

HENDRYK: I . . . what?

ESTHER: We didn't "see" each other.

HENDRYK: For five years.

ESTHER: You make it sound like we dated.

HENDRYK: You think this is all about my mother.

ESTHER: It's not *not* about your mother. Of course I think it's about . . .

HENDRYK: I think you're a dyke.

ESTHER: Lesbian.

HENDRYK: Wasn't hostile.

ESTHER: Felt like it.

DYMPHNA: *(to ESTHER)* Thought he was gone.

ESTHER: *(to DYMPHNA)* He's supposed to be.

BILLYGOAT: *(to HENDRYK)* So are you to my thoughts as food to life.

HENDRYK: *(to BILLYGOAT)* Stop it. *(to ESTHER)* I've gained twenty-four pounds.

BILLYGOAT: Or sweet-seasoned showers are to the ground.

HENDRYK: Last night on the subway I urinated. In my pants.

BILLYGOAT: And for the peace of you I hold such strife.

HENDRYK: *(to BILLYGOAT)* SHUT UP! I hate the sonnets. Boring boring boring.

BILLYGOAT: . . . as 'twixt a miser and his wealth is found.

HENDRYK: I'm BROKE! I know women who have slept with you. New York is a tiny village. Well, it isn't but I do. I work with a woman who has. Slept with you.

ESTHER: No you don't.

HENDRYK: Yes I do.

ESTHER: No you don't.

HENDRYK: Yes I do. I know you're a lesbian.

ESTHER: And how does it make you feel.

HENDRYK: Sleep with me.

ESTHER: I'm going to charge you for this visit.

HENDRYK: I'll pay twice what I paid.

ESTHER: You're broke.

HENDRYK: I'll mug someone.

ESTHER: Ba-DUM-bump.

You keep saying "sleep" with me.

HENDRYK: Sex.

ESTHER: Sleep isn't sex.

HENDRYK: Nitpicker.

ESTHER: It's interesting.

HENDRYK: Kleinian nitpicker. I think you can sleep with me, uh, have sex with me because unlike the truly great analysts of the past who had unshakable faith in the stern tenets of their discipline you and all modern practitioners of . . . well, of anything, of psychoanalysis in this instance, in our . . . um, *pickle*, conundrum, whatchamacallit, have, well, faith but no unshakable faith, no one does in anything these days, we have . . . ambivalence, it's why we tattoo ourselves.

ESTHER: What?

HENDRYK: So like those priests who wind up sleeping with children, it's not their fault, I mean we should put them in prison of course kill them probably who knows I know that's bad to say but there are days when everyone, um seems like everyone should be killed, you know? In a world in which no structure rests assuredly, with assurancy on a foundation, in which nothing comes with a metaphysical guarantee, because even, take even an old atheist like Freud, God was still *watching*, He was *watching* all the way up until so-on-and-so-forth but today, today . . . Well, take me for instance.

Only you have ever been watching me. For five years.

And nothing lasts longer than five years. Used to be, used to be . . . *ten* at least. And so abuse of your . . . of *one's* . . . wards, patients, *inferiors*, subjects. Well it's wrong but not absolutely so because there simply are no absolutes, and. The, uh.

ESTHER: I think the associative leap to tattoos is interesting.

HENDRYK: Tattoos last.

ESTHER: Your mother was tattooed.

HENDRYK: *That* again.

ESTHER: I am *absolutely* never going to sleep or have sex with you.

HENDRYK: Because I'm fat, urinate in my pants, and I'm broke. And frightening. I have a thought disorder.

ESTHER: I don't think you do.

HENDRYK: I think I do, but perhaps my thinking I do is a result of a thought disorder. If you think you have a thought disorder and you do have one, you're thinking a correct thought, in which case you don't have a thought *disorder*. So if I *don't* have a thought disorder, but think I do, *that* is a disorder, which means I *do* but then well you get the point. It's a small point. I saw a man with tattoos all over his body yesterday covering almost all his flesh like an epidermatological crisis. Now *that's* frightening. And I thought wow, the uh. Bet his skin will always smell like cheap ink. I thought, *wow*, the *pain*, he must've really enjoyed that suffering, bet he remembers every inky little needle stick. This is how he knows he's been here. Because it hurt to be. He has inscribed proof of his, well, not *existence* but . . . OK, sure, existence, sure, existence in, inscribed on his own, on his, in the only arena available to the Late Twentieth-Century Citizen seeking effectivity, historical agency: his or her skin. I cannot change any world except this small world which is bounded by my skin. I can change nothing, I can only hire a biker with a needle to bruise into my flesh "Live Free or Die."

I'm scared. I'm scared of the world.

I really want to come back to you.

Maybe I'll get a tattoo.

Pause

Ambivalence expands our options. It increases our freedom, to, to . . . tattoo. Our selves. If we wish to. To have a concept like "our selves" or "my self." Which makes us more ambivalent and more free. Which drives us crazy, and makes us desperate to find non-ambivalent things like tattoos which for all their permanence and pain serve mainly as markers of how ambivalent and impermanent we are. Or feel we are.

ESTHER: Actually tattoos are removable. Nowadays.

HENDRYK: I hate the way you introduce irrelevancies.

Pause

I have a boyfriend now.

ESTHER: That's good.

HENDRYK: He's beautiful and he has no soul. None. In nature there's no deformity but the mind. None are called evil but the unkind. Beauty's, um, good, a good thing, beauty is goodness, but the Beauteous Evil are empty trunks o'erflourished by the whatchamacallit. The Devil. As they say. I don't, I don't by the way believe that you are right that my mother named me Hendryk because it sounds like Schmendrik.

SHE WAS *DUTCH*, FOR CHRIST'S SAKE! It's a *DUTCH NAME*! *NOT* . . . um, *NOT*. BECAUSE. IT SOUNDS. LIKE SCHMENDRIK. I don't think she meant that. I think that's wrong. I think you could be, uh I could sue you for malpractice for suggesting that, for, for, implanting, inscribing whatchamacallit, for forging neural pathways in my brain. Maternal ambivalence is lethal. You ruined my life.

ESTHER: But she *did* call you Schmendrik, Hendryk.

HENDRYK: SO?

ESTHER: She called you that all the time. It's Dutch but you were born in Massapequa. Schmendrik, Hendryk. The words are practically homonymic.

HENDRYK: Homophonous, actually, is what you . . .

ESTHER: Homonym and homophone are . . . homologues. They're homologous.

HENDRYK: They're homonyms, actually, not homologues, though homophony is the precise . . .

ESTHER: But if they're homonymous then they're precisely . . .

HENDRYK: Though there is a word more precisely connoting closeness but imprecision. But I can't remember what it is. Homophones are, like . . .

ESTHER: Tattoo and taboo.

HENDRYK: No, those aren't, they're, oh ha ha.

My mom's favorite actor was Oskar Homolka. When she was angry she'd say "What have you done, Oskar Homolka?" "Listen up, Oskar Homolka!" The subtext of the last minute is "homosexual." There I beat you to it. Pissed?

All this coil is long of you.

I want back in.

Tattoos are taboo for Jews. Taboo. It's . . . TABOOOOOOOOOOOOOOOOOOooooooooooo. Like anal sex. I'm not a homosexual. I can't be. I have no talent to be. And anyway, the, uh. Anal sex disgusts me. Ugh. Anal sex. Ugh. I am filled with horror. Well that's too strong. Disgust.

BILLYGOAT: Do you know why that is?

HENDRYK: I don't know why it doesn't disgust everyone.

BILLYGOAT: But it doesn't.

HENDRYK: I don't know why.

BILLYGOAT: All sex has fragrance, and is sometimes malo-
dorous. Love like Attar of Rose overwhelms with its
fierce volatility the mephitic pungency of elimination and
waste. When two lovers are conjoining. When my cock
is up your butt.

HENDRYK: That is horribly horribly horribly embarrassing,
what you just said, and I am going to vomit.

BILLYGOAT: Shit transforms.

HENDRYK: No it doesn't. It's irreducibly revolting. And
germy. That is its essence. To revolt and spread disease.
You are very beautiful but you have no soul.

BILLYGOAT: Shit transforms when you're in love.

HENDRYK: Maybe I've never been in love.

BILLYGOAT: Maybe not.

   Pause

HENDRYK: How . . . sad.

ESTHER: Schmendrik.

HENDRYK: *(to ESTHER)* Waitaminnit.

   (to BILLYGOAT) But you love me.

BILLYGOAT: I do.

HENDRYK: But how is that possible? I mean, *look at me*? And
you have no soul. I, I'm reasonably sure about that.

You're a satyr. A Priapist. Nothing human is alien to you. It's inhuman.

BILLYGOAT: Having no soul makes a person indiscriminate. Makes it possible to fall in love with unworthy object choices, like you.

HENDRYK: But if I don't let you fuck me, you'll leave me.

DYMPHNA: I thought he was gone, I thought he terminated.

ESTHER: He asked to see me.

DYMPHNA: What's his real name? It isn't Schmendrik.

Pause

DYMPHNA: I hate him. You shouldn't let him back.

ESTHER: I won't.

DYMPHNA: Ever. Promise.

ESTHER: Ever. Banished. Be gone.

HENDRYK: I don't understand.

BILLYGOAT: I have to leave you.

HENDRYK: But that's . . . that's *crazy*. You love me so much my shit smells like Attar of Rose. I mean I can't say that without feeling nausea. But you say it does. But you're going to leave me if we don't fuck.

BILLYGOAT: Yes. Because your refusal means you don't love me. I know that's bad to say but we both know what the refusal means. You don't love me, Hendryk. And that breaks my heart. It makes me want to die.

HENDRYK: So if you leave me, you're going to die? Or are

you just going to find a boyfriend who has no problems with the smell of Attar?

BILLYGOAT: Ummmm. The latter.

ESTHER: This morning I thought the bed was full of sand.

HENDRYK: I don't understand.

DYMPHNA: Is it bad today?

ESTHER: Hi-ho hi-ho, it's off to work I go.

Yes, it's very very bad.

I want to die. God has closed my womb and I want to die. As a lesbian and a feminist and a rational progressive person and everything I am, as lucky as I am, I know it's bad to say this but I don't give a fuck. I am so fucking depressed I want to die. Die die die die die die die die. I want to have a baby. If I can't have a baby I want to die. I can't take any more of those pills, I don't want to get cancer; I don't want to superovulate I just want to have a baby so bad I want to die but I don't want cancer. But I really do want to die. I hate the baby that won't be born. I hate the five failed sperm donors. Inexplicably, I hate you. Certainly I hate myself. I can't describe the hatred I feel for the doctors who . . . I have projected the hatred I feel for those doctors and their superovulators onto my shrink and her antidepressants so I can't re-member to take my Zoloft, which I need to do but I hate her and her Zoloft for seeking to rob me of my death-desiring depression which is now the only thing left of my baby. I don't believe in God, I never did, not even a little but my hate believes in God apparently and He has closed my womb so fuck God. While my patients are

jabbering away on the couch I wish I had a big sand
bucket like kids have at the beach and I imagine myself
with a plastic shovel pouring sand in their jabbering
mouths, slowly and deliberately and seriously the way
kids do, filling their mouths with sand not just to *(to
Hendryk)* SHUT THEM UP *(to DYMPHNA)* but obviously to strangle them; I wish all the world was burnt to
a cinder, I wish I lived on the island of Montserrat. I do
live on the island of Montserrat. You know, that island
with the whatchamacallit . . . the volcano. I imagine you
calling my patients and saying "Esther is dead, Dr.
Zauber is dead, she killed herself, sorry, here are refer-
rals," they would all be shocked and sad and so forth but
also deeply gratified to have finally heard what you sound
like, to have it confirmed that you exist, *my lover*. Para-
sites. Oy. Oy. Die. Die. Oy vey iz mir. Oh woe is me.
Every morning's . . . I'm sorry, but it's only ever "Oh no
not *this* again." And know what? My complete lack of
hope is all that keeps me alive. I think that if for one
moment I felt hope, I would have the courage to kill
myself. For real.

BILLYGOAT: *(to HENDRYK)* There's always douching.

ESTHER: *(to HENDRYK)* Did you ever play on the shore
with a sand bucket?

HENDRYK: *(to ESTHER)* Why?

(to BILLYGOAT) Douching isn't foolproof.

ESTHER: Just wondering.

BILLYGOAT: Ah, well, *foolproof.*

HENDRYK: I hate that.

BILLYGOAT: What?

HENDRYK: That continental wearywise affected sophisti-
cated louche thing you lapse into. Ah well, foolproof.
Americans don't say "Ah." Ah well, foolproof. Ah well
the smell of feces. In the faubourg of Paree of my youth
we would eat it with petit pois off tiny platters of
Limoges . . . Please. You're from Dearborn. In houses all
across Dearborn mothers are teaching little boys to crin-
kle their noses in revulsion at the smell of ordure. Maybe
they don't even need instruction, maybe it's innate, at-
avistic: poo-poo, yuck. What went wrong with you?

BILLYGOAT: With love's light wings did I o'erperch that
revulsion.

HENDRYK: You're so *robust*. You don't really *get* ambivalence. The satyr which is half man, half goat should get
ambivalence but animals don't, that's why we say they
have no souls, ambivalence is the soul, it is our species
being, and against animal certitude human ambivalence
is too ambivalent to stand up for itself I guess and so,
voilà. You. I'm going to lie down now.

ESTHER: Time's almost up.

HENDRYK: *(to ESTHER)* Can I fuck you?

DYMPHNA: *(to ESTHER)* Can I fuck you?

BILLYGOAT: *(to HENDRYK)* Can I fuck you?

ESTHER: *(to HENDRYK)* No.

    (to DYMPHNA) No fucking tonight.

BILLYGOAT: Don't let me leave you. I may not have a soul

but I'm beautiful so do your soul a favor, hang on tight to me.

HENDRYK: I'm going to lie down now.

ESTHER: When you lie down on the couch you always pass out. Your efficient Resistance.

HENDRYK: Just for a . . . *(He lies down.)* For old times' sake. To what? Why resist. I never met anyone who wasn't overcome. Eventually.

The pillow always smells.

ESTHER: Many troubled heads have been laid upon it.

What about paternal ambivalence?

HENDRYK buries his face in the pillow and inhales deeply.

ESTHER: What does it smell like, Hendryk?

HENDRYK: Attar. Of Something. Nice.

Not now I'm trying to sleep.

Thank you for seeing me. Aren't I sad? Paternal ambivalence, there's no such thing as that. My father lacked ambivalence. He hated me, till he figured out how to swallow me. Which he did in three snaps of his mighty jaws and washed me down with beer. It hardly hurt. Him or me. Once incorporated I was more or less safe and more or less whole.

Though spectacularly, lipsmackingly, invincibly unappetizing.

He's asleep.

ESTHER: Hendryk.

Hendryk.

I have problems of my own.

DYMPHNA: Our inability to love one another is human-kind's greatest tragedy. Why can't people live up to their moral goodness? It's better to share. It's more pleasant to be kind. Maybe not in the moment, but immediately after. It's exhausting to despair. Love replenishes itself, day after day. It's easy to love, it's hard to refuse. Surprises are always coming. Adversity is better met by good cheer and a placid spirit. Generosity makes us free. Sacrifice lifts the soul. For the happy woman there is no terror in the night. *Lass meine Schmerzen nicht verloren sein.* Let my sorrow and my pain not be in vain. Don't kill yourself. Work. Each evening come home to me. Surely goodness and mercy will follow me all the days of my life. I love that. Surely they shall. Surely. Surely.

ESTHER: For me that word is so rotten with doubt and hesitation, it rings. It's a question in a closet.

DYMPHNA: Don't kill yourself. Work. Each evening come home to me.

ESTHER takes the keys to her office out of her purse, scribbles something on a piece of paper. She wraps the keys in the paper, puts them quietly on the sleeping HENDRYK's chest, turns out the lights, and tiptoes out.

HENDRYK wakes up as the door shuts. He looks about. He sits up. The keys fall into his lap. He opens the paper in which they are wrapped. He jingles the keys. He reads the note.

HENDRYK: Lock. Up. After. Yourself.

FINIS

So are you to my thoughts as food to life,
Or as sweet-season'd showers are to the ground;
And for the peace of you I hold such strife
As 'twixt a miser and his wealth is found:
Now proud as an enjoyer, and anon
Doubting the filching age will steal his treasure;
Now counting best to be with you alone,
Then better'd that the world may see my
   pleasure;
Sometime all full with feasting on your sight,
And by-and-by clean starved for a look;
Possessing or pursuing no delight
Save what is had or must from you be took.
   Thus do I pine and surfeit day by day,
    Or gluttoning on all, or all away.

PAINTING YOU

 WILLIAM FINN

INSPIRED BY SHAKESPEARE'S SONNET 102

ORIGINAL MUSIC BY WILLIAM FINN

ORCHESTRATION AND ARRANGEMENT
BY JASON ROBERT BROWN

CHARACTERS

PAINTER............................*Stephen DeRosa*

MODEL.........................*Jason Alan Carvell*

SONNET 102 ....*James Farmer*

A Painter sings to his Model.

> Don't move.
> Try to relax and smile.
> In a little while
> I will let you eat,
> Or I will rub your feet,
> Or I will make you feel completely at ease.

Model begins to move.

> Ah please.

Model begins to sneeze.

> No, don't sneeze.

Model sneezes.

> I will not dull you with my paint—
> Making you into what you ain't;
> Nothing I can do can make you better than
> The man
> You are.
> I paint mountains, I paint skies;
> I paint clouds in their formations;
> But I still have reservations
> About painting you.
> 'Cause when I do:
>
> It's just arms and legs!
> I capture nothing but these
> Arms and legs!
> I stand and smile and try to paint you.
> I sit and concentrate on your ass.

I paint you—
Alas—
That's it!
It's shit.
I cannot paint you,
I cannot burrow into your soul;
The parts do not make a whole
And so I quit.
Ahhhhh! I quit!

Remember
The paintings I made when we met?
Your silhouette—
Hard to forget.

The Painter sits with the Model.

But with each passing year
I fear
The more I love,
The more I am incapable of
Painting you.
But still I paint you.
I-I-I-I-I-I-I-I-I paint you.

During the ascending I's, the Model caresses the Painter. They kiss; then the Painter gets up, returns to the canvas, and doesn't paint.

But with each passing year
I fear
The more I love,
The more I am incapable of
Painting you.
But still I paint you.
I paint you.

And the Painter begins painting.

My love is strength'ned, though more weak in seeming;
I love not less, though less the show appear.
That love is merchandiz'd whose rich esteeming
The owner's tongue doth publish everywhere.
Our love was new, and then but in the spring,
When I was wont to greet it with my lays,
As Philomel in summer's front doth sing,
And stops her pipe in growth of riper days;
Not that the summer is less pleasant now
Than when her mournful hymns did hush the night,
But that wild music burthens every bough,
And sweets grown common lose their dear delight.
   Therefore, like her, I sometime hold my tongue,
   Because I would not dull you with my song.

WAITING FOR
PHILIP GLASS

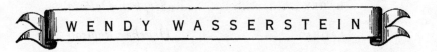

WENDY WASSERSTEIN

INSPIRED BY SHAKESPEARE'S SONNET 94

Two women are standing in an East Hampton living room. The room is obviously the home of a contemporary collector. The women are around thirty-five and extremely attractive. SPENCER wears a halter that shows off her well-sculptured body. HOLDEN wears a softer caftan, looking more ethereal. SPENCER is looking at a vase of lilies.

HOLDEN: Do you think they're happy in there?

SPENCER: I've never seen your house look prettier. These flowers are amazing.

HOLDEN: Ecuadorian lilies. That doesn't mean they're happy in there.

SPENCER: Why wouldn't they be happy? They're eating. They're talking. And everybody's here.

HOLDEN: The guest of honor isn't here.

SPENCER: He'll be here.

A couple walks by. HARRY and LAURA walk into the room.

HOLDEN: Hello, Harry!

They wear matching sweaters over their shoulders. HARRY is excessively warm. He hugs both women.

HARRY: I'm so sorry we're late. We just came from Al's little thing for Henry Kissinger. What a great event! You know my wife, Laura Little? Laura, this is our gracious host.

They shake hands.

HOLDEN: I admire your work. And this is Spencer Blumfeld.

SPENCER: *(kisses Laura)* We know each other. You look so beautiful!

HOLDEN: Can I get you a drink? Philip Glass will be here any minute.

HARRY: Who's that?

SPENCER: The guest of honor. Tonight is a benefit for him.

LAURA: Harry, he's a very important avant-garde artist. Cutting edge. He directed *Einstein on the Beach*, which I could sit through every night.

HARRY puts his arm around Laura.

HARRY: We popped over to Spain last week for the Guggenheim opening in Bilbao. I can't tell you how exciting that little museum is.

He kisses her.

LAURA: I'm training Harry to start thinking globally. It's our job to keep up.

He kisses her again.

HARRY: Everyone thinks I married her for her looks. It's not true, I did it for her energy.

LAURA: Honey, I think I'd like some water.

HARRY: No ice. Lime.

They walk into the next room.

HOLDEN: Robert Wilson.

SPENCER: What?

HOLDEN: She thinks she's here to see Robert Wilson. He directed *Einstein on the Beach*. Our guest is the composer.

SPENCER: She won't know the difference.

HOLDEN: Do you think she's a good writer?

SPENCER: If you think an overrated sex column is good writing.

HOLDEN: Harry's a very nice man but . . .

SPENCER: But you could never marry him. Not even just for five years to fulfill the prenup? Cause she'll be leaving him the day after. That's not a diamond on her finger. It's a satellite dish.

HOLDEN: I'd do anything for this night to be over.

SPENCER: You can't be cuckoo enough to think they were madly in love.

HOLDEN: Why not? It would have been nice.

SPENCER: But highly unlikely.

HOLDEN: I'm just not up for this. I look enormous and ancient.

SPENCER: I think you look great. But if you're unhappy, I'm thrilled with my eyelift.

HOLDEN: You look fabulous.

SPENCER: Our health and beauty department has done the research. When a woman turns thirty-five it's blastoff for corrective surgery. Any later you lose the skin's elasticity. I'm giving you great advice and you're not listening to me.

HOLDEN: I just wish he would goddamn get here.

SPENCER: Who? Have you invited someone else I should know about?

HOLDEN: No. The guest of honor. The artist in question. And I wish everyone hadn't just seen each other at Alan's perfect little thing for Henry Kissinger. And furthermore, where the fuck is Diane Sawyer?

SPENCER: Take it easy. I thought you said that shrink of yours is helping you.

HOLDEN: She's helping me with the memory of my mother who lowered my self-esteem by competing with me for attention from my withholding father. That has nothing to do at all with this evening being done and over.

SPENCER: I give up. I really don't know what you want.

HOLDEN: I want Diane Sawyer here. And I want Philip Glass here.

A balding man of around thirty-five comes into the room. He is not conventionally attractive but commands attention. He is compulsively eating crudités.

GERRY: You changed caterers. I hate caviar in baby bliss potatoes. Give me a cocktail frank or Swedish meatball any day. How are you, Spencer?

SPENCER: I'm terrific, Gerry. Congratulations on your marriage. I met your wife's dad in Washington the other day.

GERRY: Are you spending a lot of time with the Secretary of Transportation?

SPENCER: It was a party at Ben Bradlee's and Sally Quinn's for our September issue.

GERRY: Well you certainly caused a nice little buzz with that.

SPENCER: Thank you. I didn't know you read women's magazines.

GERRY: I read everything. But you should do more about emerging Hollywood. No one cares about Michelle Pfeiffer and her babies anymore.

SPENCER: Holden, can I get you another spritzer?

HOLDEN: I'm fine. Thanks.

GERRY: Honey, she just wants an excuse to run and tell everyone she can't believe what I just said to her.

SPENCER: I'll bring you back a Swedish meatball.

SPENCER leaves the room.

GERRY: I've never understood your interest in that woman. She's a hideous climber and everyone says she's going to be fired. That September issue was a total embarrassment. And the entire company's up for sale anyway.

HOLDEN: Are you buying it?

GERRY: Boring. It's no fun if it's just about making money. I'd rather stay home with my wife. You're looking well.

HOLDEN: Thank you.

GERRY: Kids are good?

HOLDEN: Kids are great. Kip's in Maine and Taylor's at this terrific summer camp in Cambodia. She's learning to plant rice and dig her own latrine.

GERRY: So you won't have to tip the doorman at 873 Park Avenue to do it anymore.

HOLDEN: That was an easy shot.

GERRY: You set it up.

HOLDEN: I read you bought that English publishing house.

GERRY: Now this is seriously interesting. You buy the world's largest chain of discount drugstores and nobody notices. You buy Jonathan Swift's bankrupt publishing house and Henry Kissinger's congratulating you. By the way, you should have come to Alan's little thing for him.

HOLDEN: Well I was here. Organizing my own little thing.

GERRY: I'd say it was the classiest event of the summer. The regulars like Mike and Diane Sawyer were there but there were some neat surprises, too.

HOLDEN: Diane Sawyer was there?

GERRY: And Bill Bradley, Steven Spielberg, April Gornick, and Erik Fischl.

HOLDEN: The painters?

GERRY: Alan is considered a major collector now. Rina and I ran into him at the Guggenheim opening in Bilbao. You have got to get there. You know I never thought much of Gehry's work but he has really hit his stride. But if I had to do it all over again I'd be an architect.

HOLDEN: Then you'd have to listen to other people's opinions.

GERRY: I'd hate that.

HOLDEN: I know.

GERRY: A lot of your friends were there and Harry and the sexpert. She should be sued for malpractice for those columns. I've tried those positions and they're only possible for a spastic giraffe or a lesbian hydra.

HOLDEN: Gerry, shh. They're here.

GERRY: Why do you let these kinds of people into your house?

HOLDEN: He's a friend of mine.

GERRY: She's an ex-lover of mine. That doesn't mean I have to feed her. I have to say I was very lucky. After my first marriage there was basically you and Rina. You two were the standouts.

HOLDEN: Well, at least we had the most quotable fathers. So you liked Bilbao?

GERRY: You really don't want to talk about us. Or why until tonight you've avoided meeting my new wife.

HOLDEN: I'm just waiting for Philip Glass.

GERRY: Why don't you tell your guests if they write a check they can all go home now. All they want is to be excused. We all just saw each other with Henry Kissinger anyhow.

HOLDEN: You don't have to stay, Gerry . . .

GERRY: I have to stay, I'm only here for you. *(kisses her)* Where's that guy you've been dating?

HOLDEN: He's inside.

GERRY: I heard he's a something.

HOLDEN: Developer.

GERRY: Sounds promising. What does he develop?

HOLDEN: Pennsylvania.

GERRY: You can do better.

HOLDEN: What's the matter with Pennsylvania?

GERRY: Nothing. Except Liberty Bell condos.

HOLDEN: How do you know the name of his condos?

GERRY: I pay attention. That's my business. Holden, you don't need to throw it all away on some dolt who drives a Lexus. Does he wear Gucci loafers? Cause it would kill me to see you with a guy in Gucci loafers. At least wait till you're forty.

HOLDEN: He wears Hermès loafers.

GERRY: Are you doing this deliberately?

RINA, a beautiful young woman of around twenty-two comes into the room. She is dressed in something resembling a slip.

GERRY: There you are. We were just talking about you.

He kisses her.

RINA: This is such a beautiful house.

GERRY: I think it's one of Bobby Stern's better ones. Delightful play of air and light. Holden's father had it built.

HOLDEN: It was kind of a first wedding present.

GERRY: Holden's father was a philosophy professor at Princeton. Wonderful man. Sort of my idol.

HOLDEN: He was alcoholic and married five times before his suicide.

GERRY: But he spent his life paying attention to what truly interested him. Of course I have no robber barons in my family so that was never an option for me.

RINA: These are beautiful lilies. Where are they from?

HOLDEN: Ecuador. They're much heartier than the ones from Holland.

GERRY: Holden does her own flowers.

HOLDEN: It's a hobby of mine. My daughter asked me once why I hired a man to put flowers into a vase.

They all laugh uncomfortably. A burly man in a Gucci belt and loafers comes into the room.

JOE: So where's the guest of honor?

HOLDEN: He's on his way. Joe, I don't think you know my friend Gerry Gavshon.

JOE: No, but of course I'm always reading about you. Congratulations on that Binmart deal. You're killing every discount store in my part of the country.

GERRY: We're opening next month in Moscow and Beijing. Who knew that in our lifetime we could say we made the world safe for Alka-Seltzer. This is my wife, Rina. Are you a big fan of Philip Glass?

JOE: Holden took me to see something of his.

HOLDEN: *Glass Pieces*. The Jerome Robbins ballet.

JOE: The one with those gorgeous young people going across the stage.

GERRY: That could be a lot of things.

HOLDEN: No, Joe, you're right. I know the one you mean.

JOE: Personally, I like a song that goes somewhere. But you've got to give them both credit. It was a lively show and most of the time ballet except for the jumpers can be really boring.

HOLDEN: Do you go to the ballet, Rina?

GERRY: We prefer the opera. We're going practically every free evening. I used to be intimidated but it's really very easy to pick up.

JOE: That's the way to stay young. Learn something new. Have you ever been on an Outward Bound trip?

GERRY: Spending the night alone on a mountain in Colorado. I'm from the suburbs of Pittsburgh, Joe. I know the answer. I'd never survive without take-out Chinese.

JOE: You eat a few roots and you're fine. Listen, I've been with them on Hurricane Island, I've sailed a Viking ship down a fjord, but last week I did something extraordinary. I went solo to the South Bronx for a night. Terrible neighborhood. Crack vials on the street. People you think if you look them in the face you'll never see your kids again. And I made it through. First time I've been really scared in years.

RINA: Once the baby's born I want to teach cooking at a Phoenix House in the South Bronx.

GERRY: Sweetie, they don't need to learn fat-free cooking at a Phoenix House in the South Bronx.

HOLDEN: When is your baby due?

RINA: Next March. Gerry wants a large family. I told him now that we've got the ranch even six kids is okay with me.

HOLDEN: What ranch?

GERRY: We got a little place in Jackson Hole. Around one thousand acres. And it's easy to get to if you don't rely on commercial airlines. We just pop over to Teterboro and we're there. Believe me it makes a lot more sense than driving to the Berkshires.

SPENCER comes back into the room.

SPENCER: Honey, people are beginning to start leaving. Nora told me to give you a big kiss but she had to meet Diane Sawyer, and Kathleen Turner says she had to rush out before her babysitter turned psycho.

HARRY and LAURA come out.

HARRY: We heard he wasn't coming.

HOLDEN: He's on his way.

HARRY: Honey, we're expected for dinner.

GERRY: Whose dinner?

HARRY: Just Joe and Patty. Are you going?

GERRY: He's a second-rate talent. With a gift for schmooz-ing. And she's lucky she hasn't been indicted.

LAURA: I thought they were friends of yours.

HARRY: You two know each other?

GERRY: We're acquainted. Nice seeing you again.

LAURA: Nice seeing you again. It was a great party, Holden. Please tell Mr. Glass I'm one of his greatest fans.

GERRY: Laura . . .

LAURA: Yes.

GERRY: I really enjoyed your last column.

LAURA: Thank you. Good night.

They exit.

JOE: What does she write about?

GERRY: Blow jobs.

JOE: That takes guts.

SPENCER: She can't help herself.

HOLDEN: I better go in there and tell them he's on his way.

JOE: Maybe we should invite everyone out for dinner. Nothing wrong with having lobster and white wine over-looking the ocean.

SPENCER: And we could all reenact *Einstein on the Beach*.

HOLDEN: You go ahead.

JOE: What?

HOLDEN: You go ahead. I can't leave my guests.

JOE: I wouldn't leave you at your party.

HOLDEN: No, please, take Spencer and get a lobster on the beach.

SPENCER: What are you talking about?

HOLDEN: I prefer that you go.

SPENCER: Gerry, this is your fault.

GERRY: I didn't say a word.

SPENCER: Why did you come here?

GERRY: I was invited. I wanted my old friend to meet my wife.

HOLDEN: Rina and Gerry bought a ranch where they're hoping to raise a family.

GERRY: You're not giving Rina the credit she's due. Rina graduated Phi Beta Kappa from Bowdoin. She got into Harvard Medical School.

RINA: Gerry, you don't have to tell everyone that.

GERRY: Why not? It happens to be true. And Rina's setting up the Rina and Gerry Gavshon Pediatrics Foundation.

RINA: I think I would like to go home now. I'm feeling a little tired.

GERRY: We can't leave now.

RINA: Would you drop me at home?

JOE: Of course.

GERRY: What are you doing?

RINA: My feet are hurting. I need to lie down.

GERRY: You can lie down here until the guest of honor comes.

JOE: Spencer and I will take you home.

HOLDEN: You're a gentleman, Joe.

JOE: I'll just drop her off and be right back.

HOLDEN: You don't have to.

SPENCER: Are you insane?

HOLDEN: No. I'm waiting for Philip Glass. *(She kisses SPENCER on the cheek.)* Good night.

GERRY: You just sent a perfectly nice man away.

HOLDEN: I thought I shouldn't throw myself away on a dolt who drives a Lexus.

GERRY: You shouldn't listen so carefully to everything I say.

HOLDEN: Your wife is charming. I liked her a lot.

GERRY: She gets tired. But when you total it all up she makes the most sense.

HOLDEN: A good long-term investment.

GERRY: Don't be crude.

HOLDEN: I didn't get to Bilbao. I am crude. Would you excuse me while I retrieve my party?

He grabs her by the arm.

GERRY: What the hell is wrong with you?

HOLDEN: Nothing. I just want to tell them to wait. That's all.

GERRY: It makes no difference if they wait.

HOLDEN: But our guest will come and tell us all what it's like to be an artist. What it's like to think you can make up a life that's different from your own.

GERRY: There's nothing wrong with your life.

HOLDEN: You're absolutely right there's nothing wrong with it at all.

GERRY: Let me take you to dinner tonight? After he leaves.

HOLDEN: I can't. I have a date.

GERRY: Your date just left.

HOLDEN: He's not my only date.

GERRY: So you're leaving me here alone.

HOLDEN: Good for me. Bad for you. Isn't that what you once told me in business had to be tru

GERRY: This isn't business. This is friendship.

HOLDEN: I'm tired of friendship. Good night, Gerry.

She kisses Gerry.

Thank you so much for dropping by.

GERRY: You have no idea how much I respect you.

HOLDEN: It's great news about Binmart in Moscow!

GERRY: *(suddenly yells)* Talk to me, Holden!

She takes the lilies out of the vase.

HOLDEN: These are for Rina.

GERRY: Please, you don't have to.

HOLDEN: Most likely I won't be here in the morning. And lilies that fester smell far worse than weeds. Good night.

She watches as GERRY leaves the room. HOLDEN stands up, pulls herself up straight, and walks into the adjoining room.

HOLDEN: Everyone. He's on his way.

END

They that have pow'r to hurt and will do
  none,
That do not do the thing they most do show,
Who, moving others, are themselves as stone,
Unmoved, cold, and to temptation slow—
They rightly do inherit heaven's graces,
And husband Nature's riches from expense;
They are the lords and owners of their faces,
Others but stewards of their excellence.
The summer's flow'r is to the summer sweet,
Though to itself it only live and die;
But if that flow'r with base infection meet,
The basest weed outbraves his dignity:
  For sweetest things turn sourest by their
    deeds;
  Lilies that fester smell far worse than weeds.

THE GENERAL
OF HOT DESIRE

 JOHN GUARE

INSPIRED BY SHAKESPEARE'S
SONNETS 153 AND 154
AND
THE GOLDEN LEGEND
BY
JACOBUS DE VORAGINE
(1229—1298)

ORIGINAL MUSIC BY ADAM GUETTEL

MUSICAL DIRECTION BY KIMBERLY GRIGSBY

CHARACTERS

SETH .... *Daniel Pearce*

MICHAEL .... *Hamish Linklater*

CAIN .... *Heather Robison*

SHEBA.................................... *Lisa Tharps*

GOD.................................... *Stephen DeRosa*

ABEL/KING OF SHEBA ... *Jason Alan Carvell*

ADAM/SOLOMON .... *James Farmer*

EVE .... *Jennifer Rohn*

SETH'S CHILDREN.............. *Erika Rolfsrud*

Lisa Tharps

SONNET 153 .... *Erika Rolfsrud*

SONNET 154 .... *James Farmer*

Actors, wearing glasses, pore over piles of books and pamphlets.
Erika reads Sonnet 153.

ERIKA:

Cupid laid by his brand and fell asleep.
A maid of Dian's this advantage found,
And his love-kindling fire did quickly steep
In a cold valley-fountain of that ground,
Which borrowed from this holy fire of Love
A dateless lively heat, still to endure,
And grew a seething bath, which yet men prove
Against strange maladies a sovereign cure.
But at my mistress' eye Love's brand new-fired,
The boy for trial needs would touch my breast.
I, sick withal, the help of bath desired,
And thither hied, a sad distempered guest,
 But found no cure: the bath for my help lies
 Where Cupid got new fire: my mistress' eyes.

She is puzzled. She leaves the stage. JAMES reads Sonnet 154.

JAMES:

The little Love-god, lying once asleep,
Laid by his side his heart-inflaming brand,
Whilst many nymphs that vow'd chaste life to keep
Came tripping by; but in her maiden hand
The fairest votary took up that fire,
Which many legions of true hearts had warm'd;
And so the general of hot desire
Was sleeping by a virgin hand disarm'd.

This brand she quenched in a cool well by,
Which from Love's fire took heat perpetual,
Growing a bath and healthful remedy
For men diseas'd; but I, my mistress' thrall,
    Came there for cure, and this by that I prove—
Love's fire heats water, water cools not love.

JENNIFER: That was Sonnet 154. Can we go back to 153? "Cupid laid by his *brand*"?

DANIEL fishes through various editions of texts scattered around looking for the appropriate footnote.

DANIEL: Signet Signet—"Brand"? ahh, a torch.

JENNIFER: "This *advantage* found"?

DANIEL: *(the same)* Pelican Pelican—"Opportunity."

JENNIFER: "And his love kindling fire did quickly steep"— steep? As in staircase?

DANIEL: *(the same)* Cliff Notes Cliff Notes—

HAMISH: We have university paperbacks and you bring out the Cliff Notes?

JENNIFER: I'm not too proud.

DANIEL: "Steep steep." Oh. Like tea. You dunk the tea bag in water and steep.

JENNIFER: Oh—like tea bag.

HAMISH: Tea bag? I don't understand one word of this sonnet—

DANIEL: If you read the sonnet in one swoop the meaning becomes—

HAMISH: I'm looking for the Larger Meaning—

JENNIFER: "But found no cure, the bath for my help lies where Cupid got new fire: my mistress' eyes."

HAMISH: Was Shakespeare paid to write these sonnets?

DANIEL: I don't think so.

HAMISH: Wait! Is this the hook! Royalty paying for praise from an oppressed artist? Economics? Pre-Marxist exploitation of the lower artistic classes in Elizabethan England—

DANIEL: Why?

HAMISH: Then what is this sonnet really about?

DANIEL: You are the prime example of the failure of modern education. A mind is a terrible thing to—

HAMISH: What the hell does this mean? "Love cannot be quenched—Cupid asleep by a magic spring." The world is falling apart. Bosnia—Northern Ireland—the Middle East—let's do a play about Cupid asleep? Cupid! Wake the fuck up! Art has to change the world. Art should be a call to action, not some essay on sleeping putti.

STEPHEN: This is such an old-fashioned argument. The old How can you have beauty when so much ugliness exists in the world? The old How dare you have comedy in a time of tragedy, love in a time of so much hate. It's a basically flawed argument. Art is one thing—politics is— It's not worth—

HAMISH: I refuse to do courtly sentiments of love. Art has to make some sense of life—illuminate life. That's the purpose of art. That's our duty. What's the purpose of this sonnet?

DANIEL: Could Hamish leave?

LISA: I understand what the sonnet means: I thought my love was dead but I see you and love is back.

STEPHEN: It's like Motown.

HAMISH: Bosnia. Northern Ireland. Palestine. Motown.

LISA: Is he writing this to his dark lady?

DANIEL: Cliff Notes—no—this is not one of the dark lady sonnets.

STEPHEN: But is it one of the sonnets to the mysterious young man—"the world's fresh ornament"?

JASON: That's a hook. Explore the issues of gender and race. Shakespeare torn between the dark lady and the young man—

STEPHEN: Shakespeare's torment! I can do that! Blow winds! To be or not—

DANIEL: Cambridge says nothing about gender.

JENNIFER: Or race. I have Yale.

DANIEL: Cliff Notes Cliff Notes. Sonnets 153 and 154 are not about the young man or the dark lady. Or economics. Just about love. Shut up, Hamish.

JENNIFER: Could we go on? "A dateless lively heat, still to endure / And grew a seething bath"—

HAMISH: A seething bath?

DANIEL: Cliff Notes. "Angry as in seething mad—"

HAMISH: This bathtub is angry? Perfect sense. Surrealism.

JENNIFER: "The bath footnote undoubtedly a reference to the waters of the town of Bath for the Greek original says nothing about curative powers."

HAMISH: Greek original?

DANIEL: Sonnets 153 and 154. "The original source . . . appears to be an epigram in the Greek anthology. Controversy has raged over Shakespeare's source. . . ."

JENNIFER is enraptured by DANIEL.

HAMISH: Wait. Hold on. Just hold on. Shakespeare didn't write this?—

DANIEL: Pelican Pelican: "153–154—Their authenticity has been questioned."

HAMISH: Questioned?

DANIEL: Monarch—"May have translated 153 and 154 from the Greek when he was fifteen."

ALL: *(amazed reaction)* Fifteen!

LISA: Mozart.

HAMISH: Fifteen years old? We're doing Shakespeare's homework?

ERIKA enters breathlessly carrying a bag.

ERIKA: Wait! I have—

ERIKA produces a large volume out of the bag.

ERIKA: Helen Vendler!

Cheers. All flock to the large book of Helen Vendler.

ERIKA: *The Art of Shakespeare's Sonnets,* Belknap/Harvard. Published 1997. Helen Vendler is the expert! *(reads)*

"Sonnets 153 and 154 are close in plot but not identical"—good good.

DANIEL kisses ERIKA passionately.

LISA: I love Helen Vendler!

Jennifer bursts into tears.

ERIKA: "Each is an anacreontic narrative about the unquenchability of love"—anacreontic?

HAMISH: *(reaches for a dictionary)* Chambers Chambers.

Daniel stands in a murderous rage, pulling the Chambers dictionary away.

DANIEL: The footnotes are my job. You understand that!

Everyone freezes at the tension between the two. HAMISH backs off and moves away.

DANIEL: *(brightly)* Chambers Chambers—"after the manner of the Greek poet Anacreon, sixth century B.C.—free, convivial, erotic—"

LISA: *(taking the Vendler)* "One fifty-three is Cupid's story."

STEPHEN: *(taking it from Lisa)* "One fifty-four is the lover's story; retelling the anacreontic parable becomes an exercise in hermeneutics as each personal 'application' reinterprets the phallic myth."

HAMISH: The phallic myth?

DANIEL: This is about love.

HAMISH: Then show a greater love.

HAMISH: We can make something grand out of this!

JASON: I love in the next sonnet—Cupid is the general of hot desire—

HAMISH: Make that the title. The General of Hot Desire.

STEPHEN: I want to play The General of Hot Desire.

DANIEL: *(a revelation)* Wait! General of Hot Desire. The initials spell God—

Pause

JASON: Well, God with an *H*—

STEPHEN: The *H* is silent as in 'urricanes 'ardly 'appen in 'ampshire, 'ereford or 'artford.

HAMISH: You're making it a musical about a Cupid in a bathtub?

HEATHER: And Diana a goddess.

HAMISH: No more exploitation—let her rest.

STEPHEN: I saw a Princess Di key chain.

JENNIFER: No! Diana on a larger scale—not Diana the goddess, not Diana the keychain—no—

JENNIFER and HEATHER: Diana the woman.

HAMISH: Not just Woman—but the First Woman—

LISA: Eve.

JAMES: Kicked out of Eden by a vengeful God. God! The General of Hot Desire. A god who created the universe in seven days, and then collapsed, exhausted by his hot desire—

Music. Thunder. Lightning.

LISA: Bath! I see a spring,

HAMISH: A stream,

DANIEL: A river—

ALL: The sea.

JENNIFER: Cupid.

HAMISH: Not Cupid.

JASON: Not Eros.

STEPHEN: Not Venus.

JASON and JENNIFER: Something bigger.

DANIEL: Wings!

LISA: Arrows!

ERIKA: An angel.

JENNIFER: Not just an angel.

JENNIFER and JASON and ERICA: An archangel!

DANIEL: And fit in the sonnet!

STEPHEN becomes God and climbs above them.

HAMISH becomes the archangel MICHAEL, winged like a Renaissance fresco by Piero della Francesca.

HAMISH AS MICHAEL: I am the archangel Michael. I look around heaven and see God asleep—the general of hot desire taking a breather—tossing turning dreaming vengeful dreams—

GOD (*asleep*): Disobeyed me—eat my apples—they didn't listen to me—expel them—seven days I waste creating a world for them—what do they do? First chance they get? Betray me—I wanted a world that was quiet—obedient—they had to cause trouble—the hell with them.

MICHAEL: I look down on a loveless world and see Eve and Adam, the victims of that expulsion, are still alive.

ADAM and EVE: Barely.

MICHAEL: They've had children. They live in a dark gray barren desert where a cold icy wind never stops. Eve and Adam have never spoken to each other since the day of their disobedience, the day of their expulsion. They each blame the other.

EVE: Her eyes are lifeless.

ADAM: His rimmed with red.

MICHAEL: Eve who named daylight and warmth still thinks she has the task of naming things and can't lose the habit.

EVE: Despair. Isolation. Depression.

ADAM: Shut up. Shut up.

EVE: Grief. Self-pity.

MICHAEL: Two of their sons never stop fighting on the barren gray desert.

CAIN and ABEL fight violently.

CAIN: You did it.

ABEL: You did it.

EVE: Rage. Blame. Defeat. Resentment.

MICHAEL: Adam steps between Abel and Cain and receives a blow to the heart.

ADAM falls and cries out.

EVE: *(no reaction)* Angina. Sclerosis. Scoliosis. Arterioscoliosis. Psoriasis. Halitosis. Hay fever. Rose fever. Rheumatism. Shortness of breath. Night sweats. Boils. Hemorrhoids.

ADAM: None of the above.

MICHAEL: Abel and Cain stop fighting for a moment to look at their father—

EVE: Unconscious. Gasping. Agonizing.

MICHAEL: Then resume their battle.

CAIN: You hit him.

ABEL: You hit him.

ADAM: Stop this! God! What do we do to get your attention?

GOD: Let them suffer. This universe is just a doodle. My next universe . . .

MICHAEL: Seth, another son, runs out of his cave and sees Adam unconscious on the ground, the breath seeping out of him.

SETH: Father? What are you doing?

MICHAEL: No one has yet done what Adam's now doing. The world has had everything it will ever have except—

SETH: Mother, what do we call it?

EVE: Betrayed. Money-back line. Grudges—hatred.

ADAM: No, it's more than that.

MICHAEL: They will learn to call it—

MICHAEL whispers in EVE's ear.

EVE: Death?

MICHAEL: And now the first man is experiencing the first—

ADAM: Since this was about to be the first

ALL: Death.

ADAM: I am terrified by this nameless thing. But I know this: My time on earth is over. I know there had once been water in abundance and now all was desert; I know there had been—what was the word?—and now there was no—

MICHAEL: *(whispers)* Love.

EVE: Eve doesn't hear it.

ADAM: Adam remembered love. But he could not remember the name for it was the one thing that had been named and now it no longer existed. He called it:

MICHAEL: For want of a better word

ADAM: Water!

SETH: There's got to be a spring—

ADAM: Water. God, hear me?

GOD: Get what they deserve. Eat from my Tree of Knowledge. The tree contains classified information—knowledge there is no need for you to know—I am The General of Hot Desire.

CAIN: You hit him.

ABEL: You hit him.

MICHAEL: Seth pounds the rocks trying to get water out of them—

SETH: It will help you, Father. And the pain is so great that something new is born in man—

MICHAEL: Sympathy.

SETH: God! How do we get your attention? What do we do to make you hear us?

ADAM: God, hear me?

MICHAEL: Michael does not want to disobey but Adam's pain causes him—

EVE: Anguish. Revulsion. Self-loathing.

MICHAEL: Pain.

ADAM: Water.

GOD: No.

MICHAEL: *(calls after SETH, whispers)* You—Human—there's no more mercy—but I will give you seeds from the tree that caused all the trouble—the Tree of Knowledge— take the seeds from this tree and plant them in your father's mouth and then place your father in the earth—

ADAM: *(sits up)* Bitter—bitter—this is not mercy—this is knowledge! I've already tasted this crap! What the hell have you given me? This is the taste that can never be satisfied—I don't want knowledge—I want mercy—I want mercy and you give me knowl—

ADAM falls back.

EVE: Death.

SETH: What is death?

EVE: The opposite of love.

SETH: God, hear me?

GOD: *(wakens for a minute)* Yet again they've eaten from the Tree of Knowledge? Drive them farther away from me.

MICHAEL: And the first family is expelled to an even darker desert where—

SETH: I and Abel and Cain bury our father. Cain and Abel resume their battle.

CAIN: You did it!

ABEL: You did it!

EVE: There will be a new word. Murder.

SETH: There has to be love. The years go by and out of my father's mouth grows a tree that gives me shade and some form of—

EVE: Fear.

SETH: Shut up, mother—comfort and when it comes time for my mother to die . . .

EVE: I had it all. I had Eden. I had it all.

SETH: We bury her by my father under the tree and then it came my time . . .

SETH'S CHILDREN: and we buried our father Seth beneath the tree and then my sons and daughters and their sons and daughters—we all nourish the tree until it is time to flower. And now look—there comes water. A spring bubbles up beside the tree. The tree flowers.

MICHAEL: God in his slumber smells the scent of the blossoms.

GOD: *(rage)* What is that tree? Where did it come from? That tree is knowledge? They did it again? Who gave them the seeds? How did they get it? Destroy them.

Thunder

MICHAEL: And God turns his back on the world again and lets the people who live under that tree be drowned in floods, then taken into slavery.

Music. The actors form a tree.

MICHAEL: As the years go by, the roots of the Tree of Knowledge spread silently, secretly, under the cover of earth—some branches of the tree come up in India and nurture a baby called

LISA: Buddha.

MICHAEL: In South America a god called

JAMES: Cuotemac.

MICHAEL: At the North Pole they call the gods

LISA: The Tornait—the invisible rulers.

MICHAEL: In Africa, a god called

JASON: Ifejioku—

THE OTHERS: Olokun—the god of the sea

Agbala—

Amadiora—

JASON: Ani—the owner of all lands.

GOD: Call me what you want. I still don't hear.

MICHAEL: The tree sprouts up and man keeps building things with it—trying to get God's attention. A pyramid.

JENNIFER: A statue.

HEATHER: A poem.

MICHAEL: Moses remembers a dream of the tree he's never seen. He has to get back to it—to a river he's never seen, a tree he's never known. And he frees his people to get back to that tree.

DANIEL: And David becomes king and when David dies

JASON: His son Solomon is now king.

SOLOMON: I sit beneath this tree by this river and try to write a poem on paper made from this tree with my pencil made from a twig of this tree. And when winter comes, I love this tree so much.

MICHAEL: The roots of the tree travel the earth. A sprig comes up in Africa. Solomon receives the first letter ever written from the King of Sheba.

KING OF SHEBA: My dear King Solomon, I am the King of Sheba. In Africa, my sons have all died in battle. My daughter now rules as queen. As the first gift of her coronation, she will be sent on a trip to gain knowledge.

Word has reached us that you are the wisest man in the world for you sit under the Tree of Knowledge. Please receive my daughter the Queen of Sheba and instruct her.

SHEBA: Sheba is amazed by the world. She stops when she sees the bridge over this river—a sprig of new growth pops up. She bends down to pull off a twig—she is struck down by a terrible vision.

GOD: Put those seeds back! They are not to be removed! Haven't you learned anything? How many times do I expel you from paradise?

SHEBA: I hide the seeds between my breasts.

GOD: God goes back to sleep—dreaming of the next time— the next creation—a universe filled with obedient Armadillos. Hedgehogs—

MICHAEL: *(whispers to Sheba)* Walk gently on this bridge! Walk lightly. God does not want you to have comfort, God does not want you to have peace—why can't you just obey God and be quiet and shut up.

GOD: Michael—I'm trying to sleep—

MICHAEL: *(whispers to Sheba)* A savior of the world will one day hang from a cross made out of the wood of this bridge. Tell Solomon to hide his wood. Tell him religion won't catch God's ear—

SHEBA: I gasp when I see Solomon asleep along the river.

Sings

The little Love-god, lying once asleep,
Laid by his side his heart-inflaming brand,

Whilst many nymphs that vow'd chaste life to keep
Came tripping by; but in her maiden hand
The fairest votary took up that fire,
Which many legions of true hearts had warm'd;
And so the general of hot desire
Was sleeping by a virgin hand disarm'd.
This brand she quenched in a cool well by,
Which from Love's fire took heat perpetual,
Growing a bath and healthful remedy
For men diseas'd; but I, my mistress' thrall,
    Came there for cure, and this by that I prove—
Love's fire heats water, water cools not love.

SOLOMON: I am the Rose of Sharon and the Lily of the Valleys. As the lily among thorns, so is my love among the daughters. As this tree among the trees of the wood, so is my beloved among all the world's men.

SHEBA: Let him kiss me with the kisses of his mouth for thy love is better than wine.

MICHAEL: And something happens that God does not understand. Men by themselves invent something Eve could never name. Humans have invented a fragile fantasy of their time spent in Eden.

SOLOMON and SHEBA: Rise up, my love, my fair one, and come away. For lo, the winter is past, the rain is over and gone; the flowers appear on the earth; the time of singing of the birds is come. Arise, my fair one, my General of Hot Desire, and come away.

SHEBA: Sheba remembers her vision and tells this to—

MICHAEL: Solomon who becomes terrified that it means

SOLOMON: The destruction of my kingdom. Rip this bridge out of the river and bury the wood of this tree within the deepest bowels of earth at the entrance to hell.

MICHAEL: And so I did.

SHEBA: And Sheba was on one side of the river and Solomon on the other. And soon she was gone—

MICHAEL: She conceives a child, and while there is no proof, there is the thought that the great great—many greats son of this union—will be born thousands of years from now in a small town of Mecca and his name will be Muhammad.

Music like a cry from a muezzin

SOLOMON: I often come back to watch the river that no one can now cross. Occasionally sick people are brought here; bathing in the water heals them. The priests bathe animals being prepared for slaughter—trying to get God's attention.

SHEBA: Religions grow—

JENNIFER: People make music—

HEATHER: Paint pictures—

JASON: Sculpt marble—

JAMES: Carve stone—

DANIEL: Build cathedrals.

GOD: Trying to get the attention of God—

MICHAEL: Some of the wood floated to the surface and was used to build a stable in Bethlehem. Many years go by—a child is born in that wooden place and the boy Christ becomes a carpenter working at the edge of that river.

JASON: He drinks from the river. The water is briny and salt. The river has become the Dead Sea.

JENNIFER: As Jesus saws and carves his wood, he inhales the Tree of Knowledge—

ERIKA: He conceives a notion that knowledge must become love.

JAMES: This fragile impulse must be the engine that drives the world.

GOD: *(slumbering, then waking)* Eden? Eden? It's back. . . . I waken one more time to see what has happened. I thought I had destroyed— Michael! He's no good. Yet again it's time to drive humans out of the hope of Eden. I create an angel named

ALL: Judas.

GOD: Get rid of this would-be self-proclaimed prophet. I don't want any more contact with these humans. One chance. They had their one chance!

ALL: Judas turns in Christ to the Romans for giving man hope.

MICHAEL: When Christ was sentenced to die by crucifixion, the Romans looked for wood to make a cross.

SETH: The wood from the Tree of Life breaks free of its place under the earth and floats to the surface. Pilate's men take the wood, not knowing it is wood from the Tree of Knowledge—and make the crosses.

MICHAEL: The moment of death on Golgotha is so violent that the cross sinks to the bottom of the earth.

ALL: Judas feels it, feels all hope go from the world.

GOD: Now will they learn?

CHRIST: Three days later, Jesus comes back, refusing to die. "My God, my God! Why hast thou forsaken me!" Don't you hear me? Jesus turns to Eve for the words to name what it is I'm trying to do.

EVE: The words? I'm still naming things? This damn tree. We chop it down. We carve its wood. We eat its leaves, constantly mistake knowledge for mercy—we keep constantly taking from that tree—that's all we know. All God knows how to do is expel us from Eden. Over and over. All man knows is how to try to get back. Play on wooden pipes. Sing songs—make a sonnet.

Ababcdcdefef gg.

Can fourteen lines bear so much weight?

The weight of auditioning for God?

Hoping this time he will hear us?

A symphony, a drawing, a dance, a sonnet.

These fragile inventions of man's are man's only defense against the silence of God.

And we keep trying to contact that which cannot be contacted, name that which cannot be named, define that which can never be defined. What are our tools? Something as paltry as a sonnet—

a song—

a dance—

a story—

is a hazy reminder of what we had in that garden when the Tree of Knowledge still grew alongside forests of mercy.

God, we wanted mercy and all you gave us was knowledge.

MICHAEL: God rolls over and goes to sleep.

GOD: My next universe . . . my next . . .

MICHAEL: And the sprigs from the tree grow up yet again through the ground.

Lisa sings.

Love's fire.

Pause

HAMISH: And that's it.

HEATHER: I don't buy it.

DANIEL: Isn't it rather earnest?

ERIKA: It says here Cliff Notes Cliff Notes that many of the sonnets are quote "too often marred by the Elizabethan fondness for strained conceits."

JASON: And what about Islam?

HEATHER: And I think it's anti-Semitic.

DANIEL: I think it's racist.

HAMISH: Fuck you and racism!

They start to battle. Others pull them apart.

ERIKA: No! Please! Listen: "Cupid laid by his brand and fell asleep."

HAMISH: Asleep means asleep I assume as in asleep? In Shakespeare "asleep" could mean "wide awake" Signet Signet.

DANIEL: I'm reading the Cambridge University edition.

HEATHER: I have Yale—

LISA: I have Oxford and Harvard.

DANIEL: A different edition—Signet Signet Monarch Pelican.

They throw the books as they wrestle.

GOD: *(wakens)* This is the way it's supposed to be.

The cast goes off arguing.

THE END

Cupid laid by his brand and fell asleep.
A maid of Dian's this advantage found,
And his love-kindling fire did quickly steep
In a cold valley-fountain of that ground,
Which borrow'd from this holy fire of Love
A dateless lively heat, still to endure,
And grew a seething bath, which yet men prove
Against strange maladies a sovereign cure.
But at my mistress' eye Love's brand new-fired,
The boy for trial needs would touch my breast.
I, sick withal, the help of bath desired,
And thither hied, a sad distemper'd guest,
   But found no cure: The bath for my help lies
   Where Cupid got new fire: my mistress' eyes.

The little Love-god, lying once asleep,
Laid by his side his heart-inflaming brand,
Whilst many nymphs that vow'd chaste life to keep
Came tripping by; but in her maiden hand
The fairest votary took up that fire,
Which many legions of true hearts had warm'd;
And so the general of hot desire
Was sleeping by a virgin hand disarm'd.
This brand she quenched in a cool well by,
Which from Love's fire took heat perpetual,
Growing a bath and healthful remedy
For men diseas'd; but I, my mistress' thrall,
 Came there for cure, and this by that I prove—
 Love's fire heats water, water cools not love.

BIOGRAPHIES

Eric Bogosian is the author of two plays, *Talk Radio* (New York Shakespeare Festival) and *subUrbia* (Lincoln Center Theater), as well as three Obie Award–winning solos: *Drinking in America; Sex, Drugs, Rock & Roll;* and *Pounding Nails in the Floor with My Forehead.* He wrote the screen adaptations for both plays, receiving the Berlin Film Festival's Silver Bear for outstanding achievement for his work on *Talk Radio.* His new play, *Griller,* was produced by the Goodman Theatre as part of its 1997–1998 season.

As an actor, Bogosian has been featured in films by Robert Altman, Paul Schrader, and Taylor Hackford and starred opposite Steven Seagal in the 1995 action movie *Under Siege 2.* He is best known for starring as the misanthropic radio shock jock Barry Champlain in Oliver Stone's film version of Bogosian's *Talk Radio.* In the past year he has appeared in films as disparate as Jon Robin Baitz's *The Substance of Fire* and Mike Judge's *Beavis and Butthead Do America.* He appears in Woody Allen's *Deconstructing Harry* and HBO's *A Bright Shining Lie.*

His collaborations include a 1986 album recorded with the late Frank Zappa and the recent ABC television series *High Incident* created with director Steven Spielberg.

Bogosian's plays and solos have been staged around the United States and the world. They are published, as is his novella *Notes from Underground,* by Theatre Communications Group. The screenplay to the film *subUrbia* is published by St. Martin's Press. Recently the prestigious American Audio Prose Library released selections read by the author along with an in-depth interview. The Blackbird Recording Company will release a live performance recording of *Pounding Nails in the Floor with My Forehead* later this year. Bogosian lives in New York City and has a home on the web at http://www.ericbogosian.com.

William Finn is the writer and composer of *Falsettos* for which he received two Tony Awards®: Best Book of a Musical and Best Original Score Written for the Theater. He has also written and composed *In Trousers*, *March of the Falsettos*, and *Falsettoland* for which he received the Outer Critics Circle Award for Best Musical, two Los Angeles Drama Critics Awards, two Drama Desk Awards, and a Guggenheim Fellowship in playwriting. Mr. Finn also wrote the lyrics to Graciela Daniele's *Tango Apasionado* (with music by the great Astor Piazzolla) and, with Michael Starobin, the music to James Lapine's version of *The Winter's Tale*. His musical *Romance in Hard Times* was presented at the Public Theater in New York City. Mr. Finn provided the music and lyrics for the Ace Award–winning HBO cartoon *Ira Sleeps Over* and also *Poky Little Puppy's First Christmas*. With Ellen Fitzhugh, he has written the scores for *Brave Little Toaster Goes to Mars* and *Brave Little Toaster Goes to School*. His musical *A New Brain* opened at Lincoln Center in the spring of 1998.

John Guare wrote *Six Degrees of Separation* (1990 New York Drama Critics Circle Award/Best Play, Dramatists Guild's Hull-Warriner Award, Obie), *The House of Blue Leaves* (1971 New York Drama Critics Circle Award/Best American Play, Outer Critics Circle Award, Obie), *Rich and Famous*, *Marco Polo Sings a Solo*, *Landscape of the Body* (1978 Dramatists Guild's Hull-Warriner Award), *Bosoms and Neglect*, *Lydie Breeze*, *Gardenia*, *Women and Water*, and *Four Baboons Adoring the Sun*. He wrote book and lyrics for *Two Gentlemen of Verona* (1972 New York Drama Critics Circle Award/Best Musical, Tony Award®/Best Musical) and wrote the screenplay for *Atlantic City* (New York, Los Angeles, and National Film Critics Circle Awards, Oscar nomination). He received the 1981 Award of Merit from the American Academy of Arts and Letters and in 1989 was elected a member. He serves on the Council of the Dramatists Guild.

Tony Kushner's plays include *A Bright Room Called Day; The Illusion*, freely adapted from Corneille; *Angels in America: A Gay Fantasia on National Themes, Part One: Millennium Approaches* and *Part Two: Perestroika; Slavs!: Thinking About the Longstanding Problems of Virtue and Happiness;* and adaptations of Goethe's *Stella*, Brecht's *The Good Woman of Setzuan*, and Ansky's *The Dybbuk*. His work has been produced at theaters around the United States, including New York Theatre Workshop, the New York Shakespeare Festival, the Mark Taper Forum, Berkeley Repertory Theatre, Steppenwolf Theatre, and Hartford Stage Company; on Broadway at the Walter Kerr Theatre; at the Royal National Theatre in London, the Abbey Theatre in Dublin, The Deutsches Theatre in Berlin, and in over thirty countries around the world. *Angels in America* has been awarded the 1993 Pulitzer Prize for Drama, the 1993 and 1994 Tony Award® for Best Play, the 1993 and 1994 Drama Desk Awards, the 1992 Evening Standard Award, two Olivier Award nominations, the 1993 New York Drama Critics Circle Award, the 1993 Los Angeles Drama Critics Circle Award, and the 1994 LAMBDA Literary Award for Drama, among others. Mr. Kushner is the recipient of grants from the New York State Council on the Arts and the National Endowment for the Arts, a 1990 Whiting Foundation Writer's Award, and an Arts Award from the American Academy of Arts and Letters, among others. Mr. Kushner was born in Manhattan and grew up in Lake Charles, Louisiana. He has a B.A. from Columbia University and an M.F.A. in directing from New York University, where he studied with Carl Weber. He lives in Manhattan.

Marsha Norman won the 1983 Pulitzer Prize for her play *'Night, Mother*. The play also won four Tony Award® nominations, the Dramatists Guild's prestigious Hull-Warriner Award, and the Susan Smith Blackburn Prize. Her first play, *Getting Out*, received the John Gassner Playwriting Medallion, the *Newsday* Oppenheimer Award, and a special citation from the American Theatre Critics Association. Her other plays include *Third and Oak: The Laundromat and the Pool Hall, The Holdup, Traveler in the Dark, Sarah and Abraham, Loving Daniel Boone*, and *Trudy Blue. Marsha Norman: Four Plays* was published by Theatre Communications Group. She also wrote book and lyrics for the musical *The Secret Garden*, for which she won the 1992 Tony Award® and Drama Desk Award. Her first novel, *The Fortune Teller*, was published by Random House in 1987. Ms. Norman has received grants and awards from the National Endowment for the Arts, the Rockefeller Foundation, and the American Academy and Institute of Arts and Letters. She has been playwright-in-residence at Actors Theatre of Louisville and the Mark Taper Forum in Los Angeles, and has been elected to the American Academy of Achievement. She serves on the Council of the Dramatists Guild, and is the recipient of the Literature Award from the American Academy and Institute of Arts and Letters. With Christopher Durang, she chairs the playwriting department of The Juilliard School.

Ntozake Shange is the author of *For Colored Girls Who Have Considered Suicide/When the Rainbow is Enuf*, *Spell #7*, *A Photograph: Lovers in Motion*, *Boogie Woogie Landscape*, and an adaptation of *Educating Rita*. She has also written several novels: *Sassafrass, Cypress & Indigo* (1982), *Betsy Brown* (1985), *Liliane, Resurrection of the Daughter, I Live in Music, Whitewash, and If I Can Cook, You Know God Can*. She has authored the book and lyrics for *Betsy Brown*, a rhythm and blues opera commissioned by the New York Shakespeare Festival with music by Baikida Carroll. Ms. Shange is also associate professor of drama and English at Prairie View A&M University in Texas. She has received a National Endowment for the Arts Fellowship, a Guggenheim Fellowship, and an Obie for her adaptation of *Mother Courage and Her Children*. *For Colored Girls Who Have Considered Suicide/When the Rainbow is Enuf* received an Obie, the Outer Critics Circle Award, an Audelco Award, and the Mademoiselle Award. She was the recipient of the Lila Wallace Reader's Digest Writers Award from 1992 to 1995 and was the Heavyweight Poetry Champion of the World from 1991 to 1993.

Wendy Wasserstein received the 1993 Outer Critics Circle Award and a Tony Award® nomination for *The Sisters Rosensweig*. Her play *The Heidi Chronicles*, awarded a grant by the Kennedy Center Fund for New American Plays, was first performed in the Seattle Repertory Theatre's New Play Workshop series and was later produced by Playwrights Horizons. *The Heidi Chronicles* earned her the 1989 Pulitzer Prize, Tony Award®, and Susan Smith Blackburn Prize, as well as the New York Drama Critics Circle, Drama Desk, and Outer Critics Circle awards. Other plays include *Uncommon Women and Others* (Phoenix Theatre, 1978); *Isn't It Romantic* (produced by Playwrights Horizons); and a musical, *Miami* (with Jack Feldman and Bruce Sussman). She has written screenplays for *House of Husbands* (with Christopher Durang) and *The Object of My Affection*, based on the novel by Stephen McCauley. For PBS Great Performances she has written adaptations of John Cheever's *The Sorrows of Gin*, as well as *Kiss, Kiss Darling, Drive She Said*, and her own *Uncommon Women and Others*. For Turner Television she adapted *The Heidi Chronicles*, which received a 1996 Emmy Award® nomination for Best Television Movie. Her books include *Bachelor Girls*, a collection of essays (Knopf); *The Heidi Chronicles and Other Plays* and *The Sisters Rosensweig* (both Harcourt Brace & Company), and *Pamela's First Musical*, a book for children (Hyperion). She is a contributing editor for *New York Woman* and has contributed to *The New Yorker, The New York Times*, and *Slate* magazine. She graduated from Mount Holyoke and the Yale School of Drama. In 1993 she received the William Inge Award for Distinguished Achievement in American Theatre. Her play *An American Daughter* was produced by Lincoln Center Theater in 1997.

for New American Plays, was first performed in the Seattle Repertory Theatre's New Play Workshop series and was later produced by Playwrights Horizons. *The Heidi Chronicles* earned her the 1989 Pulitzer Prize, Tony Award®, and Susan Smith Blackburn Prize, as well as the New York Drama Critics Circle, Drama Desk, and Outer Critics Circle awards. Other plays include *Uncommon Women and Others* (Phoenix Theatre, 1978); *Isn't It Romantic* (produced by Playwrights Horizons); and a musical, *Miami* (with Jack Feldman and Bruce Sussman). She has written screenplays for *House of Husbands* (with Christopher Durang) and *The Object of My Affection*, based on the novel by Stephen McCauley. For PBS Great Performances she has written adaptations of John Cheever's *The Sorrows of Gin*, as well as *Kiss, Kiss Darling, Drive She Said*, and her own *Uncommon Women and Others*. For Turner Television she adapted *The Heidi Chronicles*, which received a 1996 Emmy Award® nomination for Best Television Movie. Her books include *Bachelor Girls*, a collection of essays (Knopf); *The Heidi Chronicles and Other Plays* and *The Sisters Rosensweig* (both Harcourt Brace & Company), and *Pamela's First Musical*, a book for children (Hyperion). She is a contributing editor for *New York Woman* and has contributed to *The New Yorker*, *The New York Times*, and *Slate* magazine. She graduated from Mount Holyoke and the Yale School of Drama. In 1993 she received the William Inge Award for Distinguished Achievement in American Theatre. Her play *An American Daughter* was produced by Lincoln Center Theater in 1997.